W9-BKP-903

COMMUNAL SOCIETIES IN AMERICA
AN AMS REPRINT SERIES

THE DUNKERS

AMS PRESS
NEW YORK

THE DUNKERS

A SOCIOLOGICAL INTERPRETATION

BY

JOHN LEWIS GILLIN, A. M., B. D.

SUBMITTED IN PARTIAL FULFILMENT OF THE REQUIREMENTS
FOR THE DEGREE OF DOCTOR OF PHILOSOPHY

IN THE

FACULTY OF POLITICAL SCIENCE,
COLUMBIA UNIVERSITY.

New York
1906

Library of Congress Cataloging in Publication Data

Gillin, John Lewis, 1871-1958.
    The Dunkers.

    (Communal societies in America)
    Thesis, Columbia University.
    Vita.
    Bibliography: p.
    1. Church of the Brethren--History. I. Title.
BX7815.G5 1974   286'.5   72-8248
ISBN 0-404-11002-9

Reprinted from the edition of 1906, New York
First AMS edition published in 1974
Manufactured in the United States of America

AMS PRESS INC.
NEW YORK, N. Y.   10003

CONTENTS.

PREFACE.

This paper is an attempt to apply the principles of sociological theory to the interpretation of the denomination of Christians variously known in early history in Germany, sometimes as Pietists, because most of them had originally been Pietists, often as Anabaptists because they baptised those who had been christened when infants, or, again, as Dompelaers, from the fact that their mode of baptism was immersion. Today they are popularly known by the various names, Dunkards, Dunkers, Tunkers, but among themselves as Brethren, or officially as German Baptist Brethren. Their popular cogneman today, Dunkers, is simply the anglicised form of the German noun, derived from the old German verb "tunken", *to dip*, which corresponds to the modern German verb "taufen," and means what our anglicised Greek word "baptists" means. By their very name, therefore, the Dunkers are to be classed as baptists.

From the sociological standpoint they must be classified as a voluntary, cultural association, whose purpose was the promotion of certain doctrines and customs. It was one of the constituent societies of the larger, half feudal, half civil, social unit, the province of Wittgenstein. Therefore, from the standpoint of the historical study of society, the Dunker church belongs to that stage called civilization, or Demogenic Association, as Professor Giddings has called it. Its origin lay within the military-religious subdivision of that stage, the greatest part of its history within the subdivision called the liberal-legal, and the latter part within the economic-ethical. Nevertheless, within these narrow limits historically, the Dunker church represents in its history all the steps found in the development to be observed in the evolution of any society.

The method of approach might have been strictly sociological, were it not for the fact that the Dunker church began its development in Europe, but was interrupted in its history there, and had to start again from the beginning in America. Therefore, the study of the movement in Europe will be largely a study of social origins, and only in a minor degree of social development. On the other hand, while the origin of the movement in America must be noticed, because it originated there independently of the movement in Europe, the major part of attention will be given to the steps in the evolution of the Dunkers in social population, social mind and social organization.

The multiplication of the Dunker population from a small company of discouraged members fleeing from the evil conditions in Crefeld, Prussia, and settling in Germantown, Pennsylvania and vicinity, to a great company of more than one hundred thousand people, and its expansion from the eastern part of Pennsylvania along the natural routes of travel into all the agricultural parts of the United States will be traced, and the causes noticed.

Then the evolution of the social mind of this sect will be traced from the mental and practical resemblance that was based upon the like response to stimulus, which living under similar circumstances in Germany had produced, on through concerted volition, which resulted in the purposive organization.

Then, the evolution of the organization will be traced from the first spontaneous association of the simplest kind up through the various stages of development that led to a firmly compacted organization with an increasingly complex composition and a clearly defined constitution.

Lastly, the influence upon them in every way of the democratic society in which the Dunkers found themselves, as the country developed about them and population increased, and democratic ideas were disseminated, will be noticed.

In the last chapter a summary of the processes described in the previous chapters, will be made.

Besides the particular acknowledgments made in the foot notes and the bibliography, I wish to acknowledge special indebtedness to Professor Giddings, for help and inspiration received from his books and from lectures in Columbia University; to Professor Robinson for kindly criticisms on certain portions of the paper; to Professor McGiffert of the Union Theological Seminary for help received from his lectures on the period of church history in which this study falls; to Professor Martin Grove Brumbaugh, of the University of Pennsylvania for valuable suggestions as to sources and literature on the history of the Dunkers; and to Professor L. L. Garber, Professor of English in Ashland College, Ashland, Ohio, who has read the paper in manuscript, and given me the benefit of his good judgment on matters of literary form and statement.

PART I THE DUNKERS IN EUROPE

CHAPTER I

HISTORICAL INTRODUCTION

Long before the time of which history gives us any definite knowledge, various races of men had been meeting, perhaps mingling, in the valley of the Rhine. Investigations in ethnology and anthropology have given us hints of great prehistoric movements in western Europe, which resulted in the congregation there of several different kinds of people. It was a movement similar, in many ways, to the later barbarian migrations.

There are evidences that the neolithic population of, at least, western Europe was composed of what is known as the Eurafrican race, which, Sergi thinks, originated in Africa and spread over Europe, but which, others think, originated in Europe, and thence spread across to Africa. This Eurafrican race was differentiated into two branches, the Mediterranean and the Baltic, both longheaded, but the one dark and the other light, the one having spread over southern and western, and the other over northwestern Europe. *

Some time later a wedge of population, Aryans in language and culture, but mainly Eurafrican in physical type, with its base in Russia and its point in the British Isles, pushed itself through between the Mediterranean and Baltic branches of the Eurafrican race, and imposed its language and culture upon the people in its path, or drove them to the fastnesses of the mountains.

* Sergi, "The Mediterranean Race," *passim.*

It is probable that a second wave of Aryan people swept over this first one, but with its main direction further north, creating the Scandinavian speech and culture, but probably affecting the population of the Rhine valley only slightly.

Later still there was a third invasion of Eurafrican Aryans, who imposed their language and culture upon the population they found, and possibly amalgamated with the Eurafricans with which they came in contact in the Rhine countries. These spread throughout the region assigned by Caesar to the Celtae, or Gauls, the country between the Garonne and the Seine rivers.

Finally, there was probably a fourth migration of Aryans, Eurasian in physical type, who spread west from Hallstatt throughout the region between the Rhine, on the one hand, and the Marne and Seine, on the other, which was assigned by Caesar to the Belgae. This people had become mixed, to a certain extent, with the Germanic peoples beyond the Rhine. *

By Caesar's time there were four distinct kinds of people in western Europe, the Aquatani, southwest of the Garonne river, the Belgae, northeast of the Marne and the Seine, the Celtae, between them, and the Germani, to the east of the Rhine. † These represented the various peoples, spoken of above, that had swept in from the east and south one after the other, and which formed the basis of the modern populations of western Europe.

According to Tacitus, some of the Germans, before his day, had crossed the Rhine into Gaul. At that time probably they had extended east to the Vistula. The boundary between the Germans and the Roman provinces

* Isaac Taylor, "Origin of the Aryans," Chap. 2.

† "Gallic War," 1: 1.

was the Rhine and the Danube. * The tribes of the Germans, as the people east of the Rhine were called, pressed by the Slavic peoples to the east, or moved thereto by the growth of population within their own borders, surged out over the borders into the Roman provinces, south and west, for centuries. On the other hand, both Caesar and Tacitus tell us of migrations of tribes that lived west of the Rhine to regions east of that river. These movements made the population of the Rhine districts very complex. During the barbarian invasions of the Roman Empire this complexity was still further complicated. †

Step by step, owing to pressure of foreign foes and the pressure of their own population, the tribes were consolidated into confederacies, or leagues, temporarily, for the most part, for the purposes of defence, until in the fifth century, under the leadership of the Franks, the various tribes east and west of the Rhine were united into a single nation, which, with various vicissitudes of fortune, continued for a number of centuries. The Holy Roman Empire, which developed out of the Frankish kingdom, continued to be the one bond of political unity that held together the small states that had grown up on the basis of the former tribal divisions.

One must not conclude, however, that the political unity acheived through the extension of the Frankish rule, or the Holy Roman Empire, served to effect the amalgamation of the various elements within them, to any great extent. For on the whole, the characteristics of the races that occupied western Europe in the days of Caesar and Tacitus can be traced in the peoples that dwell to-

* "Germania," 1.

† On the whole subject in detail see Mommsen, "History of Rome," Eng. trans. 4: 255 f.

day in their respective regions. * Naturally, therefore, in the Rhine valley, the Celt and the Teuton existed, as they still exist, side by side. They were never fused into a new type, as were the Teutonic Saxons and the Celts of Britain by the coming of the Danes.

Furthermore, the inhabitants of the Rhine valley were not permanently united even politically. The strong Frankish kingdom did not hold together long enough to completely socialize the component peoples. With the accession of a line of weak kings, and the rise of feudalism it broke up into many fragments. Throughout the Middle Ages western Europe was practically a political chaos. The Protestant Reformation made more complete the political disintegration of the already tottering Holy Roman Empire by further accentuating the social heterogeneity. With the exception of France, there was no strong nation in western Europe down to the time of Napoleon. †

Thus, the races that had come into southwestern Germany had never been fused into a single people. Political, economic and religious conditions at the beginning of the eighteenth century reflected the social heterogeneity of the population of those regions considered as a whole.

The nature of the population determined the nature and development of the social mind. If into any population there has entered a variety of elements, the social mind cannot be the same as in a population of no, or only slight, admixture.

It is generally recognized that the Celtic type of mind differs from the Teutonic. Instead of being fused into

* Ripley, "Races of Europe," Chaps. 6, 18.

† Robinson, "History of Western Europe," p. 148 f; Bryce, "Holy Roman Empire," p. 14 f, edition of 1904.

a new type, as they were in England under the influence of the Dane, here in the Rhine valley we find them both, side by side, just as we saw the two races were there in close proximity, without having been amalgamated into a demotic unity.

In like manner, the different varieties of social mind among the Teutonic tribes in western Germany were not completely fused. Even to this day there is the type of mind characteristic of the Swiss German, the Bavarian, the Saxon, the Prussian, etc. Thus, there was a difference of social mind among the elements of the population of southwestern Germany as a whole, analogous to the difference in race.

All these different tribes and races responded to stimulus in much the same way. The migrations show this, as well as many of their common customs. Yet, even here there was a difference between the Celts and the Germans.

In mental and practical resemblance they were less alike. For example, the various German tribes respond'ed more slowly in motor reactions than the Celtic.* Their emotional qualities, intellectual processes, types of disposition and of character were different in the two peoples. † To a less degree this was true of the various subdivisions of the same race. It is most significant that the Reformed religion won in just that part of Germany that had the largest admixture of Celtic blood,—along the Rhine from Switzerland north,—while the Lutheran obtained its hold on the more thoroughgoing Teutons. The Reformed faith was more logical. Its propositions were the outcome of deductive reasoning to a greater degree than the Lutheran. On the other hand,

---

* Caesar, "Gallic War," 2: 1; 3: 10, 19; 4: 5, 13, etc.

† Ibid, 1: 1, 30, 31, 40, especially, 6: 11-24; Cf. Tacitus, "Germania," 28 f.

the Lutheran faith, as interpreted by Luther, was a religion rather than a theology, and its theological state-
ments were the result of an inconsistent compromise between Catholic and strictly Protestant elements, based,
not on the logical requirements of its premises, but upon the practical necessities of political and ecclesiastical
policy.

Furthermore, it was in the Reformed Church, for the
most part, that the sects arose. The cold logic of its
theological positions made it impossible for that church
to tolerate the sectarians.

Moreover, the Celts and the Germans recognized the
fact that they were different. If evidence of this is
required, it is to be found in the wars that the Germans
and the Belgae, on the one hand, and the Germans and
the Helvetii, on the other, were continually waging against
each other during the Roman occupancy of Gaul. * These
differences and the mutual recognition of them by each
race continued down to our period, owing to the fact that
there was no strong political and social agency to
accomplish the assimilation of the two elements. The
continuance of petty states, instead of the consolidation
of them into a political unity, the constantly disturbed
conditions of society in these regions, the lack of good
means of communication and the mutual jealousies of
rival princes and parties, ecclesiastical and political,
made for the continuance of a clearly recognized consciousness of kind.

Naturally, concerted volition, the condition of mind
prerequisite to co-operation, was impossible, except on a
few lines, among the people of southwestern Germany at
the close of the seventeenth century. It required the
stimulus of a great common danger, such as the tyranny

*Caesar, "Gallic War," 1:1, 30, 31, 40.

of Ferdinand II, or the oppression of Louis XIV, to bring them to a common purpose. Thus, the evolution of the social mind of southwestern Germany, as a whole, was not far advanced. Even in each state it had not progressed beyond the stage of formal likemindedness.

In like manner, the social organization of the people in the Rhine valley in Germany was incomplete. As there was no developed social mind in that region considered as a whole, so there was no all-inclusive social organization. There was but a chaos of petty states nominally united under the Holy Roman Empire. The consolidation of the states of the region occurred as late as 1870.

Moreover, in each state the organization had developed only as far as might be expected from the description given of the development of a social mind.

Where likemindedness is sympathetic, or formal, rather than rational, and where, consequently, the social action is impulsive, whatever social organization exists is coercive in its relation to the individual. This generalization is well illustrated in the social organization at this time. Prussia, the Netherlands, and Wittgenstein were the only states that allowed freedom of organization and individual liberty of religious opinion. Only such religious organizations were permitted in other parts of the country as were not at variance with the religion of the state. A coercive attitude was assumed by most rulers towards the individual and each constituent society. The task at hand was to unify the discordant elements of the population. The governing classes were trying to unify their society by enforcing uniformity in religion and politics. It was this coercion in religion that gave birth to the sectarian movements. Forgetting the interests of the governed, and imagining that their own interests must be the interests of all, the

rulers forced a reaction against their policies by the
coerced classes, who were just now coming to a consciousness of their rights.

Such was the condition of society in the upper part of
the Rhine valley, as a whole, in the period in which this
study falls. The population was made up of elements
that had come down from earlier times, which had never
been amalgamated into a racial unit. The social mind of
the region as a whole existed only in its elements. There
was very little common social purpose, and the only
semblance of a social organization was the Holy Roman
Empire. Of social organizations of a smaller scope there
was a multitude. But these had not developed any
further than the military-religious stage of civilization.
This monograph therefore, is a study of the origin and
development of a constituent society in an integral society
that had arrived at the stage of development known as the
military-religious stage.

In order to understand the early development of this
society it will be well to look more carefully at some of
the social conditions that prevailed in the Rhine Valley
at the time of its origin.

Three phases of these conditions were of special importance: (1) the reaction against the Protestant scholasticism of the period; (2) the general character of the
sects of that time; and (3) the local conditions which
existed in the Rhine-lands and stimulated emigration.

1.   THE REACTION AGAINST SCHOLASTICISM.

Out of the conflicts of the Reformation two distinct
tendencies emerged among the Protestants. Both were
found in the Catholic church before Luther; both were to
be found even in Luther himself. The one was the

scholastic, the other the mystical. The latter became identified with Pietism in our period, while the former was characteristic of the Lutheran and Reformed orthodoxy. Luther's theory of justification by faith is anything but scholastic. But, strange to say, Luther, especially in his later days, laid himself open to the charge of confusing correct doctrine with faith. He does not explicity identify saving faith and orthodoxy, but in order to oppose successfully the claims of the Catholics in regard to the authority of tradition, he was led to emphasize the authority of Scripture, and, in order to defend himself, on the other hand, against the "fanatical" claims of the extremists among the Protestants, he felt it necessary to oppose to their claims the Bible as the standard of doctrine. * This was the easier for him to do, because apparently he was not conscious that in so doing he was giving utterance to anything inconsistent with his oft-repeated assertion that the Word of God is not a *book*, but the message of God's forgiving love in Christ. Yet from the point of view of his controlling principle, this was a mistake, and opened the way for his followers to identify correct doctrines with saving faith. In the later editions of his *Loci Communes*, Melancthon expresses the same view. It is a well-known fact also that each edition of the *Loci* became more scholastic. This scholastic orthodoxy came to official expression in the Lutheran church in the Formula of Concord (1577.) In the following years such theologians as John Gerhard, Calovius and Quenstedt brought it to its complete development. The Scriptures were no longer, as they were with Luther, primarily helps in one's Christian experience, but *"dicta probantia"* for the doctrines as set forth in the confessions. Nay, more, they had in themselves a

---

*See Luther's Works, Erlangen edition. 7:34

magical power, similar to what was supposed to reside in the bread and wine of the Eucharist, viz., the power to regenerate the soul of him who read them. * The Formula of Concord was now looked upon as a complete body of divinity, assent to which constituted saving faith. The duty of reverent theologians was to comment upon it and explain it, but not to change it. For purposes of interpretation it stood above the Bible, for it contained the complete body of saving truth, while the Bible was used only to confirm it by furnishing proof texts. † Thus a dogmatism far more narrow and oppresssive than that of the Catholic church was fastened upon the Protestants.

The same thing took place in the Reformed church. It was all the easier there, because Zwingli was a humanist to begin with, and was not so great a religious genius as Luther. Little by little the scholastic method had been growing in favor with the Reformed theologians. In their controversies with the Socinians and the Arminians and with the theologians of the school at Samur, they pushed their dogmatism to as extreme a form as the Lutheran thelogians. All the discussions were scholastic in method. This scholastic dogmatism found official sanction in the Canons of the Synod of Dort (1619), and in the Formula Concensus Helvetica (1675). So it came about that henceforth in this branch of Protestantism, orthodoxy was considered a condition of salvation.

The results in both the Lutheran and Reformed churches were the same. Attention was directed to pure doctrine to the partial disregard of the Christian life. The

* See Dorner's "History of Protestant Theology," Eng. trans. 2:203 f.

† See especially, Harnack, "History of Dogma," Eng. trans. 7:168 f. I have received the most help on this subject from the unpublished lectures of Prof. A. C. McGiffert of Union Theological Seminary, of New York.

emphasis on orthodoxy served to exhaust in fruitless controversy energies that should have been applied to quickening the moral life of the people. It was heresy, not lack of spirituality, not immorality, for which men were excommunicated. Conduct was less important than creed. The natural tendency of this emphasis was to stifle in both leaders and people the fresh, evangelical spirit of the Reformation. Religious and ethical considerations had to give way to the all important question of orthodoxy. If men were good, it was because of other factors. Accordingly there resulted a widespread deadness in the churches.

Another result was that Christian love and tolerance could not develop. Zeal for orthodoxy had as its corollary hatred of heresy and the persecution of heretics. For example, because of the slight difference of doctrine between them as to the "real presence" of the body and blood of Christ in the Eucharist, the Lutherans and the Reformed were at emnity at a time when there was every reason for them to unite against a common foe. For the same reasons unseemly quarrels took place within each of the two great Protestant bodies. Within the Lutheran church the Philippists and the strict Lutherans divided on questions of doctrine, with the result that the strict Lutherans drew up the Formula of Concord against their enemies the Philippists. Within the Reformed church the orthodox party was set over against the Arminians and the theologians of Samur. Besides these main divisions in Protestantism, there were minor ones, which stood out with a similar zeal against the claims of the orthodox parties. Indeed so important was orthodoxy considered, that persecution became a common occurrence. For no other reason than refusal to assent to certain theological dogmas, thousands of men and women were killed as heretics. *

Against this scholastic theology of the seventeenth century two movements developed. The one was Pietism; the other Illuminism. With the latter we are not concerned here, as it was a later development, and did not affect the circle of society we purpose to study. On broad lines, it may be said that Illuminism was a phenomena of the upper classes; Pietism of the lower. The former was the protest of the educated; the latter of the masses. Pietism was the product of the combination of the mystical tendency that the Reformation brought over from Catholicism, † with the practical, individualistic spirit of the Reformation. ‡ It had long been felt by many people that there is something more in religion than a harsh and barren dogmatism. This feeling became more marked as orthodoxy became more pronounced in the churches. The religious spirit awakened by the Reformation could not be satisfied with the intellectualism of the theologians.

Moreover, there had been lacking from the very first days of the Protestant revolt, both in Germany and in Switzerland, parties with strong separatistic leanings. These parties found in the scholastic dogmatism of the churches additional reasons for separation from them. They represented the protest of the people of that day against the growing Scholasticism. And when to all this is added the influence of the spirit of the modern age,

* See the accounts of the persecutions of the Mennonites in their great "Der Bluetige Schau-Platz, oder Martyrer-Spiegel." In this day it is hard for one to believe that good men and women could have been so cruel.

† Ritschl has the credit of making this clear in his "Geschichte d. Pietismus."

‡ Later it combined with Separatism, which was also a popular movement against the scholastic dogmatism of the time.

the strength of the reaction against Scholasticism is easily understood. Scholasticism was mediaeval and its presence in the Protestant churches was a survival. It satisfied neither the religious, nor the scientific needs of the day. Against its pretensions to satisfy the former, Pietism and Separatism, in large part, were revolts.

2. GENERAL CHARACTER OF THE PROTESTANT SECTS.

Very early in the history of Protestantism sects had begun to appear. In fact, they had existed in Catholicism before the Protestant revolt. The Protestant sects originated partly in reaction against Scholasticism, and partly as a result of the belief in the freedom of the individual conscience, a belief that was involved in the Lutheran Reformation. In the early period of Protestantism, the separatists were simply ultra-Protestants. But when Scholasticism had fettered the living religious life in the Lutheran and Reformed churches, the separatists discovered in an emphasis upon conduct, over against the emphasis of the orthodox upon dogma, a new and mightier weapon of defense against the attacks of the latter. Among these separatistic sects those that have an interest for us are the Anabaptists of Zurich who organized themselves while Zwingli was still alive, under the leadership of Grebel, Blaurock, Manz and Hubmeier; the Mennonites, a group composed of the Anabaptists of the Netherlands, who came under the influence of Menno Symons after 1536; the Labadists, who derive their name from Jean de Labadie, and originated in 1668; the Pietists, who were not a sect, but represented a tendency that originated with Philip Jacob Spener in 1670, when he began to hold in his Lutheran congregation *Collegia Pietatis*, or meetings where simple Bible truths were discussed for the purpose of encouraging practical piety;

the Quakers, ascribing their origin to George Fox an English weaver's son, who spread to Holland and Germany; and, lastly, the Dunkers.

All of these were Separatists, except the Pietists, and consequently were organized bodies. Although their principles tended in that direction, in the beginning the Pietists were not sectarians, but counted among their numbers Catholics, Lutherans and Reformed. Later many of these joined the different bodies of separatists, while the rest of them united with the state churches. *

Each of these sects had its own peculiar doctrines, but all had certain common characteristics. In general they agreed on the following: (1) the rejection of infant baptism; (2) the necessity of regeneration; (3) the separation of the "regenerate" from the "unregenerate" in matters of conduct, such as dress, amusements and education; (4) emphasis upon practical piety rather than upon correct doctrine; (5) opposition to certain policies of the state, such as, armed self-defence, the use of the power of the state in the interest of the church, the union of church and state, the requirement of the state that the citizens bear arms, take the civil oath, and hold office under the government; (6) opposition to the use of force in self defence by the individual; (7) the theory of a "Bible-Christianity," that is, that the organization of the church and the life of the individual Christian should be modelled upon the Bible, or, as the best interpretation of the Bible, upon the organization of the early church, and the life of the early Christians; (8) opposition to the state churches on the ground that they were a spiritual "Babylon." †   These characteristics were in part the result of

---

*See "Chronicon Ephratense" Eng. trans. p. 1.

† All these were not true of Pietism in the days of Spener, and many of them were never true of it. Spener often defended the Lutheran church

a reaction against the scholastic dogmatism of the churches, in part the result of an extreme radicalism, and in
part, the result of a reaction against the intolerable social
conditions about them. These sects were recruited for the
most part from the lower classes of society, from the comparatively uneducated. Consequently, their doctrines
have to do more with conduct than with dogmas, and they
are interested in church organization and church rites
rather than in theology. *

3. Conditions in Germany that Favored Emigration.

At the beginning of the eighteenth century conditions
in the German states along the Rhine favored the emigration of the lower classes of the population. In the
contests between France and the other states of Europe,
with which Louis XIV was engaged in war during most
of his reign, the Rhine countries were the battle ground.
Across them marched and counter-marched the contend-
ing armies. On the one side of them was France, a
united nation with Louis XIV at its head, a king of no
mean abilities, and of boundless ambition. On the other
side was the Holy Roman Empire, so weak that it could
not be depended on to defend its members against the
aggressions of Louis, while the individual German states
were so small that they could not protect themselves.

Moreover, there was no effective German unity. The empire was but a loose federation, without efficient common
tribunals, and without the ability to make the unity effective by coercion. There were some three hundred small

against the charge of being "Babylon," and upheld the claim of the state
to use its power to defend itself and to help the church. See "Bedencken"
1:341. Nevertheless, there was present in Pietism the tendency to Separatism.

* This was true of the Pietistic movement in general. See Dorner,
History of Protestant Theology," 2:205 f.

German states between the Alps and the Baltic, each of
which was practically independent of the others. Mutual
jealousies prevented their unification, or even their co-
operation, except in the presence of a great common
danger. * They either were at the mercy of a strong
power, like France, or were mere pawns in the game of
politics that France and the Empire were constantly playing. For example, the Palatinate was ravaged by the
armies of France in 1674 in order to prevent the enemies
of Louis,—the Elector of Brandenburg and the Emper-
or,—from using its resources to supply their troops
against him. In 1680, without further reason than his own
ambition, Louis seized the free city of Strasburg, and
took possession of some places in Alsace, Loraine and
France Comte. In the same year he began that series of
political crimes that he called "reunions," whose purpose
was to add to France parts of the territories of these
Rhine countries.

In 1685 the Simmern line of Palatinate rulers died out
with the death of Elector Karl. It was succeeded by the
Neuburg line in the person of the Elector Philip William.
This gave Louis an opportunity to interfere in the affairs
of the Palatinate. He at once set up a claim for Elizabeth
Charlotte, a sister of the last Simmern Elector Palatine.
She had married the Duke of Orleans, the brother of
Louis XIV, but at the time of her marriage had signed
away all her feudal rights to the Palatinate, and now was
most bitterly opposed to the claims made in her behalf by
Louis. The new Elector was forced to appeal for aid to
the Empire. The emperor not being able single-handed
to checkmate Louis, formed the League of Augsburg in
1686, with himself, the kings of Spain and Sweden, as

* See Bryce, "The Holy Roman Empire," 1904 ed., p. 394 f. Henderson,
"A Short History of Germany," 2; 219 f.

princes of the Empire, the Electors of Saxony and Bavaria, the Circles of Swabia, Franconia, Upper Saxony
and Bavaria, the Elector Palatine and the Duke of Hol-
stein as its signers. In 1688 Louis decided to attack the
Palatinate, and thus strike terror into the hearts of his
enemies. The devastation of the region was one of the
most brutal on record. A hundred thousand people were
forced to leave their homes, large numbers of whom
perished; more than forty towns and villages were destroyed, and the fertile Valley was turned into a desert. *
Periodical devastation of the Palatinate continued until
Louis made peace at Ryswick in 1697. In this treaty
there was inserted a clause, since famous as the
"Ryswick clause," which resulted in the Protestants
being despoiled of their churches in the interests of the
Catholics, and the beginning of religious strife that lasted
for years. This war was followed by that of the Spanish
Succession (1701–1713). The Rhine-countries during the
greater part of these prolonged conflicts,—indeed, since
the opening of the Thirty Years' War,—were between
the upper and nether mill-stones.

Furthermore, the internal political conditions of these
small German states bore heavily upon the common
people. In many cases their officials were in the employ
of Louis XIV, or of some other great potentate. The
princes for the most part ruled solely with reference to
their own pleasures, rather than to the welfare of their
subjects. The taxes levied upon the peasants were so
burdensome that they could scarcely make a living, while
the ruler lived in a luxury patterned after that of the
French court. There was no such thing as political
liberty in the modern sense. The people had no part in

* See Dyer and Hassel, "Modern Europe," 4:55 f. And especially Haeusser "Geschichte d. rheinischen Pfalz." 2:766 f.

the government. Feudalism had broken down, but no
strong government had yet risen to reduce the chaos to
order, and to lay the foundations of political liberty.

The political situation was complicated by the intimate
relation of the state and the church. Since the Peace of
Augsburg (1555), in theory the religion of the prince had
determined the religion of the country. This gave rise
to many political disturbances. The strife between Catholics and Protestants was still keen. Each side was constantly looking for an opportunity to make inroads into
the territory of the other. The religious situation was
complicated further by the fact that there was the same
reciprocal hostility between the Lutherans and the Cal-
vinists as existed between the Protestants and the Catholics. The Palatinate had been Lutheran until Frederick III, (1559-1576), joined the Reformed church. His
successor, Louis VI., (1576-1583), reintroduced the Lutheran faith, while John Casimir, (1583-1592), was Reformed. The Neuburg line (1685-) was Catholic. Up to this
time the Palatinate had been a refuge for the persecuted
elsewhere. * The first elector of the Neuburg line, Philip William, was tolerant in religion, but he was unable to
preserve his Protestant subjects from the intrigues of
the Catholics. His son and successor, John William, was
under the influence of the Jesuits, and began a systematic oppression of the Protestants, which ended in the
Catholics getting possession of most of the Protestant
churches and in their driving the greater part of the
Protestant people into exile. The same policy was adopted by the next Elector, Charles Phillip (1716-1742). †
These rulers were simply following the fashion set by

* Kuhns, "German and Swiss Settlements of Pennsylvania," Ch. 1 gives
a very good outline of the religious conditions in the Palatinate at this time.

† For details see Haeusser, "Geschichte d. rhein. Pfalz." 2: 786 f.

Louis XIV. His persecutions of the Huguenots had forced more than two hundred thousand to emigrate. In all these small states, opposition to the orthodoxy of the Lutheran and Reformed churches had resulted in the formation of sects which were persecuted by the rulers at the instance of the national churches. For example, the Swiss Mennonites, who had enjoyed toleration within the Palatinate up to the time of the Catholic Neuburg rulers, were now forced to flee. These persecutions in the states along the Rhine stimulated emigration among the persecuted. They made settled and quiet industry impossible. Life was insecure, employment precarious, and suspicions were rife. These persecutions had made the hostility between the classes of society more marked, and destroyed that feeling of unity which makes people strong, and holds men to their native land. In the period of Huguenot persecutions, many of the latter had found religious liberty in Prussia, England and America. This emigration had set the example that was soon to be imitated by many other sects. As early as 1683, the persecuted Mennonites had begun to migrate to Penn's New Colony. Already in 1677 Penn had been on the Continent in the interests of the Quakers. From 1683 he and his agents were at work in the states along the Rhine, advertising the religious freedom of his colony. In this way the influence of persecution in stimulating emigration was supplemented by the positive inducement of the promises of religious liberty in the New World.

These political and religious conditions made economic distress inevitable. The constant wars had drawn off the men from industry to battle. Some never returned; some were disabled for life. The devastation of the Palatinate in 1688 had made a hundred thousand beggars, and ruined the industry of the country for years. The Palatinate is only the most notable example of what happened all along the Rhine valley. * Commerce was dead, for war severed the trade routes, and industry was at a standstill. Agriculture was a long time in recovering. The peasantry was burdened with most oppressive taxes, and in addition subjected to feudal services. † Furthermore, there had been a series of bad crops, and the hard winter of 1708 killed the vines.

Altogether the situation in the Rhine countries at the opening of the eighteenth century was such as to promote the emigration of the lower classes. Unstable political conditions, religious intolerance, economic disasters at home, and glowing promises of a land where all these conditions were reversed had the effect of loosening the ties that bound the Germans to their native land, and of stimulating that passion for wandering that has been so often noticed as a characteristic of this people, in spite of their intense love of home and Fatherland.

*See the evidences in Sachse, "The Fatherland," in Pennsylvania German Society Proceedings, 7: 124.

† See Kuhns, "German and Swiss Settlements, etc." p. 20.

CHAPTER II.

The Dunkers' Doctrines: ⊐ Their Origin.

The Dunker church was organized to realize certain ideals that had taken shape in the mind of Alexander Mack. This organization made necessary the further development of certain doctrines and the modification of the reasons for holding the original doctrines. That is to say, the composite nature of the population of southwestern Germany, determined the origin of certain doctrines, which, from the nature of the circumstances that suggested them, had to do with church and state. That fact determined that the ideals should be social in their nature. In turn these ideals made it necessary to have a society in which they could be realized. However, no sooner did such a society exist, than there arose the necessity of defending its existence, and of unifying its membership upon a policy and a faith. These exigencies demanded for the society an organic and statute law, the authority of which was unquestioned by opponents, and which could serve as the basis of unification for the society. This law was found in the Scriptures of the New Testament interpreted by the history of the primitive church, as that history was then understood. The necessity of defending the doctrines held in opposition to those of the state churches, and of unifying the new society made necessary the tremendous emphasis upon *obedience* that is the Alpha and the Omega of Mack's thought. Therefore, in order to account for the origin of the Dunker church it will be necessary to understand how the ideals that demanded its existence came into being.

(a) *The Doctrines:*

What, then, were these doctrines? Naming them in the order of their probable origin they were as follows:—

1. *The Christian life* is not an unethical life of correct opinion on matters theological, but a life of piety, i. e., of good works, begun by obedience to the command of Christ to be baptized, or, at least, the wish to obey that command. Baptism is followed by regeneration. This life of piety is continued by obedience to all the commandments of Christ. Here Mack, the only Dunker writer from the early period, does not define closely.

2. This position naturally includes the Dunker doctrine of simplicity of life, especially of *dress*.

3. The doctrine of *Christian perfection* was not held as firmly by Mack as by Hochmann and many others of his friends. However, he believes in it as a dogma taught by Scriptures.*

4. *Marriage* is permitted by God, but it is a lower estate than celibacy.

5. *The church* is a holy institution composed of those who have been regenerated and who manifest it by obedience to all the commandments of Christ.

6. The means whereby the church shall be preserved a holy institution of pious people is *the Ban*, as described in Matthew 18.

7. *The ministry* of this church is composed of men having Scriptural qualifications, chosen from its ranks by the congregation under the direction of the Holy Spirit. They should not be highly educated.

8. The initiatory rite of the church is *baptism* of adults only, by a threefold immersion in water. This involved the rejection of infant baptism and also of any mode other than a trine immersion.

9. *The Lord's Supper* is for those only who have shown by a pious life of obedience to Christ that they are regenerate. It is a full meal eaten in the evening, instead of a

* See "A Plain View, etc." Question 32.

morsel of bread and a sip of wine taken in the forenoon, and includes, besides the Communion, the rite of Feet Washing, in obedience to Christ's commandments in John 13.

10. *The organic law* of this church is the Scripture, especially the New Testament. This contains full and complete provisions for the organization and rites of the church. It also contains the statute law of this society, the church, obedience to which law is the condition of membership. Therefore, the supreme duty of the Christian is obedience to all the commandments of Christ.

11. *The state* is the institution ordained of God for the exercise of such powers of government as do not interfere with the conscience of each individual under its jurisdiction. Here the doctrine is entirely negative.

12. The doctrine of the state gave them the negative doctrine of *Non-Resistance*; i. e., refusal to bear arms in defence of one's country. Later it was extended to include refusal to protect one's self against violence.

13. The doctrine of the state also logically included the Dunker doctrine of refusal to take a *civil oath*.

These doctrines, noted individually above in order to show the probable order of their genesis, and to call attention distinctly to each point emphasized, may all be included either under three heads, viz., (1) the doctrine of the Christian life, (2) the doctrine of the church, (3) the doctrine of the state; or, even under two, (1) the ideal of society, and (2) the ideal of membership in that society.

With these conceptions dominant in Mack's thought there was but small place for strictly theological doctrines. What he had were survivals for the most part. At a few points they touched his conceptions as determined by his ideal of society. Thus, Mack's conception of the Gospel, the Christian life, and Sin were the result partly of his early training and partly of his dominating conception of the ideal Christian society, and therefore they had assumed a prominence not accorded to other theological doctrines, equally familiar to him. But Mack, and with him the Dunkers, were not theologians. Their interest was practical and ecclesiastical, not speculative.

God was thought of as the great lawgiver and judge.

The Gospel was conceived of as the revelation of the Christian law.

The Christian Life was one of strict obedience to the Christian law. As he conceived it therefore, man is on probation; he is not saved in the present, but is being tested to see whether he shall finally be saved.

Faith and *love* were simply *obedience* to the law.

Man was created sinless, but became corrupt through the fall of Adam. But man's will has not been impaired so that he is unable to choose the good. By obedience he can purify himself from this corruption.

Mack's *conception of sin* is not clear. He does not define "corruption". But from the fact that he says that infants who die without baptism are saved by the merits of Christ; that man became "corrupt" and "unclean" through the disobedience of Adam; that he cannot re-enter paradise until "purified" by Christ, and that what man needs is regeneration; it seems that he means metaphysical corruption. On the other hand, when he says of the effect of the Fall of Adam on man, that "man became puffed up and in his own conceit, desired greatness and power", and, that man can purify himself from this depraved condition by obedience to God's commands and by submitting his reason to the will of God, it seems that he means by "corruption" only ethical, personal guilt. Evidently Mack had no clear conception of sin. He used terms that show he was inconsistent. However, it is quite clear from the fact that he had but small place for the work of Christ, that the ethical conception is the one that controlled him. Obedience is the all important duty, as he saw it.

Salvation is future. By continued obedience to God's law, man finally shows himself worthy of salvation. If faithful to the end, he will be saved in heaven, the glories of which are described in a very materalistic fashion.

The only important points in Mack's *eschatology* are his belief that Jesus is soon to apper as judge and king, and that lost men are finally to be restored. However, it should be said that Mack does not believe in the thousand years' reign, a belief current in certain Anabaptist circles, and he thinks that the doctrine of final restoration of the lost should not be preached to sinners.

It should be noticed in this connection that the Dunkers put all the emphasis of their thought, not upon these theological doctrines, but upon the doctrines that had risen in protest against the life and practices of the orthodox churches. Hence, what the Dunkers called "doctrines" were not doctrines in the strict theological sence at all. They were, for the most part, protests against abuses that had grown up in the practical and ecclesiastical spheres of life. In other words, they were social in their nature. They had to do, not with dogma, but with conduct. They related, not to speculative thought, but to life, and church organization and rites.

(b) *Their Origin*:

The doctrines of the Dunkers were the result of their reaction upon the conditions of life and the facts of experience. We shall be able to understand better the genesis of the doctrines of the Dunkers, if we look first at the origin of the more general sectarian principles.

The complexity of the social composition mentioned

above gives us the starting point of our exposition. The material environment had determined a composite population in most of the states of southwestern Germany. The breach between rulers and ruled, feudal lord and serf, pastor and flock was wide. The small courts were aping the luxurious court of France. In order to do so, the rulers had to make the taxes of the people heavy. Both in the getting and in the spending of the money, the ruling classes widened the social chasm between themselves and their subjects. Naturally the heaviest burdens fell upon the humblest class.

By an unfortunate circumstance, the three tolerated religious were identified more or less closely with the ruling, instead of with the subject, classes. Most of the nobles belonged to the orthodox churches. The pastors of these churches were generally looked upon as belonging to the upper classes. Naturally, the interests of the court were the interests of the pastors of the dominant churches, for it was to the state that the religious authorities had to look for protection from heretics and sectarian enemies.

Another circumstance of the religious situation contributed to the social separation of the religious leaders from the people. In the period following the Reformation under Luther, the energies of the leaders of the tolerated religions had been absorbed in theological debate, which however, was of interest chiefly to learned men. This emphasis upon theology led most pastors, as well as the theologians, to neglect that aspect of religion which the common people could understand, and in which they might have taken an interest; viz., the cultivation of the religious and moral life. This had two results. Upon the less earnest Christians it had the effect of narrowing their interests in religion either to a perfunctory ceremonialism, or to the brutal pleasure of stamping out heresy by persecution. Upon the more earnest souls, on the other hand, it had the effect of weakening the ties that bound them to the church, and of driving them to the Bible and extra-ecclesiastical sources for the spiritual help they desired. Naturally the former class was the larger. These conditions produced a situation in which the slightest stimulus was sufficient to provoke a reaction by the more serious-minded against the lifeless formalism and the cold intellectualism of orthodoxy. Such a stimulus was at hand in the persecutions of this people by the orthdox churchmen.

Here, then, were in conflict two ideals, which at bottom were the outgrowths of a social difference in the population. The one ideal was that presented by orthodoxy with its harsh intolerance of anything that suggested heresy. This, for the most part, was the ideal of the upper social classes. Over against this was set the ideal of the more serious-minded part of the Christian population. This party consisted mostly of members of the lower classes of society. Again, within each of these parties were infinite gradations due to unequal response to the ideal, or to the presence of a slightly modified ideal. To this complex situation was due the origin of the many sects that characterized this period. They were social organizations formed by a like response to certain doctrines. The doctrines were the result of the conflict of diverse elements in a heterogeneous population. The heterogeneity was due to the physical character of the country.

These were the social conditions out of which grew, for example, the ideals of Hochmann von Hochenau. He was only one of a number of men who appeared in that part of Germany and in Switzerland with ideals that dif fered from those held by the orthodox churches. He here deserves special notice because his case is typical, and also because of his relation to Alexander Mack. Hochmann had been a student at Halle, where he was "awakened" under the influence of the Pietist, Francke. Hochmann was one of the most influential of the many mystical, separatistic Pietists of the time. He had come to Schwarzenau in 1698 because of a severe persecution that had broken out in Hesse-Darmstadt and Frankfort against the Pietists and the Enthusiasts. Here he lived as a hermit in a little hut, from which he would often go out upon long journeys to preach. From 1700-1711 he was absent on a pilgrimage to western and northern Germany, "as a preacher of a living, internal, but also separatistic Christianity as opposed to external ecclesiasticism (Kirchlichkeit) and dead orthodoxy."* On these journeys Mack was one of his traveling companions. And from a comparison of the teachings of these two men it is easy to draw the conclusion that Mack was an apt disciple.

Hochmann was forced, while in prison at Detmold in 1702, to write out for the Count of Lippe-Detmold a confession of faith. His doctrines according to it may be summarized as follows: (1) Upon the main points of Christianity he is in accord with the orthodox faith. He believes "in one, eternal, sole, almighty omnipresent God, as he has revealed himself in the Old Testament as the God of Abraham, Isaac and Jacob, but in the new Covenant as Father, Son and Spirit." About God he does "not find it necessary to dispute or criticize very

---

*Goebel, "Geschichte d. Christlichen Lebens," Bd 2, s. 818. To Goebel more than to anyone else I am indebted for much that is of interest to us in the history of this period. Dr. H. G. Brumbaugh drew my attention to his importance for anyone who would understand the conditions of the time in which the Dunkers arose. Dr. Brumbaugh's section on Hochmann is an excellent epitome of Goebel's chapter.

much," but considers it "better to submit one's self to
him and experience his inward working, for it is by the
inward workings that the Father reveals the Son and the
Son the Father through the mighty workings of the Holy
Spirit, without whom nothing can be attained in godly
things. This only is eternal life, that one properly acknowledge this one God." To show what he means by
this he says that he believes the "well known Ausellic
creed."* (2) He believes that "baptism is for adults only, since not one word can be found in the Scriptures of
an express command by God or Christ for the baptism
of Children." He insists that there should be just as
plain a command for infant baptism as there was for cir-
cumcision under the old Covenant. (3) He believes that
"the Lord's Supper was instituted only for the select
disciples of Christ, who by the renunciation of all worldly things follow Christ in deed and truth; and not for the
godless children of the world, who today are admitted to
the love feast." (4) He believes in Christian perfection
(Vollkommenheit). He does not claim to have reached
perfection, but he believes that "one may be sanctified
not only forensically, but also perfectly, that is, really,
(nicht allein gerecht sondern auch vollkommen geheiligt),
so that no more sin will remain in him." This he believes,
because of the testimony of Scripture. "This perfection"
he explains, "must be effected internally, i. e. mystically,
within the soul through the Son of the living God, and a
spiritual image of Christ must be won by us. Where
this does not occur in this life, men cannot attain unto
the immediate vision of God—intuition, (Anschauung),
since without holiness no one can see God, for he who has
the hope of attaining unto the intuition (Anschauung) of
God must purify himself, even as he is pure; 1 John 3:3."

* I am unable to find anywhere any reference to such a creed.

(5) He believes that "Christ alone, as head of the church, can appoint teachers and preachers, and qualify them for their positions. This Christ does through the office of the Holy Spirit." (6) He believes that government (obrigkeit) is a divine ordinance to which he willingly submits in all civil matters, but he refuses to acknowledge that those who struggle against God's word and oppress his conscience have any rightful authority. Further, he does "not believe that the *essentia magistratus politici* are necessarily Christian (dass sie ein Christ sey), because the Turk and the Pope are true authorities, but they are not Christians, and are doomed soon to be superceded by the glorious Christ, whose coming is so near at hand." (7) He believes in the "final restoration of damned men." This he believes, because of the Scriptures, and also, because "for one not to believe it would reflect on the power of Jesus Christ as Savior." *

Other beliefs held by Hochmann, which do not appear in this confession, were, (1) that all organized churches or sects are a Spiritual "Babylon", and that a mystical, Pietistical kind of Christian life independent of all organizations is the kind that pleases God; † (2) that marriage is a less holy estate than the celibate life. He taught that there are five different kinds of marriage: (a) An entirely bestial marriage. This is between two persons who are not the children of God. This is an impure estate, and cannot be made holy by the external act of the minister. By such marriages God's name is profaned. Instead of being married by the religious officials, such people should be united only by the civil authorities.   (b)

---

*For a facsmile of the Confession together with an English translation see Brumbaugh, "History of the Brethren", p 75 f. Goebel also gives a part of it in his "Geschichte d. Christlichen Lebens", Bd 2, S. 820 sq.

† Goebel, 2:818, 819.

An honorable, but yet an entirely heathenish, and impure marriage. This sort is not so bad as the first, yet in God's sight it is impure, since the parties are not in the covenant with God. This sort is by the permission of God, as all sinful deeds are, but not by the foreknowledge and will of God in Christ Jesus. The difference between this species and the first mentioned, Hochmann does not make perfectly clear. However, the inference may be drawn from what he says as to the first kind that this second kind of marriage differs from the first in that it is not entered into by the persons concerned, from purely carnal motives. (c) A Christian marriage, in which both parties are Christians, and whose purposes are not impure, but that they may have children for the glory of God. (d) A virginal marriage, in which two persons wholly betrothed and devoted to God and the Lamb become united with one another in the very purest, virginal love of Christ for no other purpose than that they may serve God in Christ without intermission, and in the pure, clear love-spirit of Jesus may be united to the eternal bride-groom of the soul, that they may be helpful to each other in such holy union of love unto perfect salvation by fighting the fight of faith together and striving together in united prayers, and then may render some assistance to each other according to the necessities of this life here on earth. As examples of such he cites instances given in Gottfried Arnold's "Primitive Christianity", and also the example of Joseph and Mary. This sort, doubtless, was a spiritual marriage. In such marriage two persons do not have sexual intercourse, but they are married simply for the spiritual advantages that comes from companionship. However, Hochmann says that they should not live together without a marriage ceremony by the proper officials, in order that no scandal may arise. (e) Marriage with Christ alone, the pure Lamb. This is the most perfect grade in the married state. When a soul betroths itself alone to God and the Lamb, and recognizes Jesus alone as its true husband, and has thus wholly betrothed and offered itself up as a bride to Christ, there the highest grade of glory in the Kingdom of Christ will be attained by a soul.*

This is all the more interesting, because we shall hear echoes of it hereafter. Especially significant are his beliefs concerning baptism, the authority of the state, the Lord's Supper, Christian perfection, and the offices of the Holy Spirit in the choosing of ministers of the Word. His position on marriage did not have an abiding influence on Mack. His doctrine of final restoration has significance for the earlier history of the Dunker movement, but the belief soon died out among them.†

I have noticed Hochmann's positions thus fully because of their influence on Mack, the founder of the Dunkers.

The rise of the doctrines of the Dunkers is a further and better illustration of the working of the social processes just noticed in the explanation of the rise of the more general sectarian principles.

Environment and historial conditions together had produced, a mixed and socially diverse population in the Rhine countries. There was no place in Europe where the conditions were more favorable to heterogeneity. The one place in the southern part of that valley, where, in 1700, a person was safe from persecution for conscience, sake, was Wittgenstein. It was not the most fertile land in Europe, but it was as fertile as the adjacent parts, and its other advantages offset its economic disadvantages. Thus, while it did not possess economic conditions fav-

---

*Goebel, 2:822 f. I have translated quite fully and almost literally.

†"Chronicon Ephratense," p. 245 f.

orable to a mixed population, the religious conditions there favored the assembling of a religious population that were in harmony on general principles, while divided on certain specific doctrines. The social composition, thus brought about, was such that general cooperation was possible in only a few matters. The differences, on the other hand, among the elements of the population were so many, and became so marked on close acquaintance that differing ideals were bound to appear through conflict and selection. For example, those who became Dunkers were first Pietists. But the social composition at Wittgenstein was such that there was no unity among the Pietists upon certain important points, such as, baptism, the ban, the form of the Lord's Supper and Feet Washing. Reacting on these conditions, Alexander Mack conceived of a certain definite ideal for the reformation of the Christian church. This ideal included the conception of specific doctrines as well as a definite programme by which the ideal could be realized. It was in response to this suggestion and ideal that the Dunker sect took form.

How these doctrines took definite shape in Mack's mind remains to be noticed. In general, this occurred through a process of conflict and selection. The heterogeneity of the population in Wittgenstein forced upon Mack and his fellow believers a recognition of mental and practical differences, and of differences of beliefs and standards, and compelled them to compare and choose. This precipitated a conflict of beliefs and standards, which could result only in the birth of new ideals, or in the strengthening of those already borrowed from an earlier time.

Naturally, the first ideals to arise out of this situation were negative, for they arose in opposition to the policy

of the party in the church socially unlike the Dunkers.
They were religious, for religion was the predominant interest of serious-minded men at that time.   And they
were ecclesiastical, rather than theological, for the people, who later became Dunkers, uneducated for the most
part, had no interests in the speculative questions of the
day, but were greatly concerned with practical questions
of church polity, organization and conduct.   Moreover,
the ideals that thus arose in reaction against the policies
and practices of the state churches, were social in that
they arose out of social conditions and had to do with social organization.   In particular these doctrines arose as
follows:

The *ideal of the Christian life* grew up in reaction
against bad moral conditions that resulted from the
church's prolonged dogmatic controversies and the consequent absorption of interest in theological discussions.
These discussions were not such as to enlist the interest
of the common people.   Since, therefore, they were not
interested in theology, and since they were a serious-
minded folk, their interest must have some object.   Such
an object was suggested by the condition of the life and
conduct of some members of the churches.   Thus, the
ideal of the Christian life that may be called Pietistic
arose.   This ideal was already in existence when Mack
and others became dissatisfied with the Reformed and
Lutheran churches.   They came to it doubtless through
a social reaction similar to that just described, and
adopted it, because it met their needs, and, because it
was an ideal held, for the most part, by their own social
class.

The insistance of the Dunkers on *plain dress* is, in part,
attributable to their doctrine of the Gospel as the law of
the Christian life. *   In part it is to be explained by their

* See 1 Tim. 2:9, 1 Pet. 3:3.

imitation of sects that had preceded them. But, more profoundly, it was due to their feeling of unlikeness to the people that formed the membership of the tolerated churches. On the part of the learned and great, it was a period of elegance and over refinement in dress. † Ordinary people could not afford to dress in the prevailing expensive fashion. They naturally felt that when wrong views of religion and ethics and a taste for fine clothes were combined in the same persons, especially when those persons were their persecutors, the elegant apparel must be as wrong as the immorality and the persecuting spirit.

The ban is similarly to be accounted for. Historically, we should say that its adoption by the Dunkers was due to, (1) the application of the principle, that life should be conformed to the moral ideals of the New Testament. * This led naturally, by an interpretation of certain passages in St. Paul, to insistance on separation from the world, which could be accomplished only by the enforcement of the ban. Its adoption was due, (2) to historical connection with such sects as the Mennonites, who held to this doctrine. But more fundamentally, it grew out of opposition to the loveless and sometimes immoral lives of those members of the Lutheran and Reformed churches by whom the Pietistic sects were persecuted. The Dunkers knew that there existed no sympathy between themselves and the noble churchmen that oppressed them with taxes and rents, who cared nothing for the welfare of the poor, when their own interests were at stake, and who lent the power of the state to the persecution of their humbler brethren. Especially alien to them were the clergy, educated, sound in doctrine, but often

*For example, Rom. 12:2, Mt. 18:15—18.

†See Schultz, "Das Haeusliche Leben im Mittelalter, etc." S. 221 sq.

un-Christian in life, interested in theological disputes rather than in the spiritual welfare of their people, hating those who were not members of their church, salaried from the oppressive taxes levied upon their poor parishioners, and often upon those who were not members of their flocks, and persecuting with the strong arm of the law those whom they could not convince with their logic.* It is little wonder that the Dunkers called the churches to which such men belonged a spiritual "Babylon". It was but natural that they insisted on the ban in order to prevent their church from having within it such men as composed the membership of the churches that persecuted them. Thus, the ban was fudamentally an expression of consciousness of kind, which in turn reflected heterogeneity of the social population.

The consciousness of kind likewise explains the opposition of the Dunkers to a paid and educated *ministry*. It was at the hands of such a ministry, that they had experienced their persecutions. Such a ministry, therefore, must be wrong. Everything that was connected with such a ministry and differentiated it from the Dunkers, must have, in their opinion, contributed to make its members godless persecutors. For the most part, the Dunkers themselves were uneducated, and hence, education must have made their persecutors what they were. If so, education for the ministry is wrong.

How shall we explain the *mystical* and *ascetic tendencies* that characterized the Dunkers in the early period of their history? These tendencies, as Ritschl has pointed out, had their roots in the Middle Ages. He finds that the tendencies present in some of the monastic orders bore fruit in Protestantism. He is right when he sees in these tendencies a reversion to type. He notes that the

*See Mack, "A Plain View, etc." p 22, 88, 89.

tendency to mysticism was present in Lutheranism itself.*
There can be no doubt that the ideal of life held by a
large element in the Catholic church, expressing itself in
monastic mysticism, and striving after ecstatic communion with God, and that the monastic asceticism that strove
to find rest and peace in the denial of matrimony and other ordinary ways of life, or in the monastic community of
goods, made a strong appeal to the common people in the
Protestant churches and sects as well as to those in the
Catholic church. Especially was this true in an age
when turbulent passions and changing customs, wars
and oppressions made men feel that their Helper was
afar off. These tendencies, appealing to men's desires
for a short cut out of their miseries, spiritual and material, found ready acceptance in such a time as we are now
studying.

But after all this is said, the question that confronts
us is, Why did men revert to the type? When we examine
social conditions in periods in which mystical and ascetic
tendencies were in the ascendant, we find poverty, oppression and great insecurity of life and property. Back
of these conditions we find heterogeneity of population.
Mysticism and asceticism have risen in those classes upon whom the burdens of life have pressed most heavily.
Hence, whether in the first centuries of Christian history
or in the eighteenth, these features of religious life have
resulted from the reaction of people upon environment
created for them by complexity of the population. In other words, they are social products.†

It was noticed above that most of the points in *the theo-*

---

*"Geschichte des Pietismus," 2: 3, sq.

†See Moeller, "History of the Christian Church," 1:356; Weingarten,
"Der Ursprung d. Monchthum," ZKG. I. 1 and 4, Goth. 1877; Also in
"Rael-Encyclopaedie," 10:758 sq.

logy of the Dunkers were simply the theology of their orthodox opponents. How did it happen, it may be asked,
that the Dunkers adopted some of the doctrines of their
opponents while they dissented from others? Of the beliefs that they had in common with the orthodox churches
several things are to be observed: (1) These doctrines,
or beliefs, related to points of theology proper rather
than to ecclesiastical procedure or matters of practical
life; (2) Being theological doctrines, they had comparatively little interest for this untheological people. These
points of theology had been taught them in their child-
hood, and, as they had no connection with specific social
differences, they never became points in dispute. The
Dunkers, consequently, who were not systematic think-
ers, simply retained them without examination. (3) These
doctrines had no connection with their social life, as did
those points in which they dissented. Therefore, they
were not forced to reconsider them. (4) They did not
enter into the ideals, response to which created the Dunker church. They had no relation to the ideal of a social
organization.

The *rejection of infant baptism* by the Dunkers can be
explained historically, that is to say, in terms of the
principle of imitation. Obviously, however, another
generalization must be invoked to account for the rejection of infant baptism by those who first rejected it,
and I think also to fully account for its rejection by the
Dunkers. This other generalization is more fundamental. Those who first rejected infant baptism did so because they felt the unlikeness between themselves and
those that practiced it. Of course, when they had rejected it, they appealed to Scripture to sustain their contention, because all Protestants invoked the binding force of
the Scriptural text. The case of the Zurich Baptists is

in point. They rejected infant baptism primarily, not because they knew of the rejection of it by some earlier sect, but because they felt that there was a greater likeness between those who refused to practice it than between themselves and the Reformed church at Zurich. Social conditions first made them different in various ways. Then they began to proclaim their views. Thereupon the main body of the Reformed party, with the aristocratic element supporting it, felt the difference also, and decided it could better afford to cut off the dissenters than to alienate "the substantial people." So the dissidents were cast out.*

Doubtless, imitation of historical precedents that had come to their knowledge, accounts in a measure for the rejection of infant baptism by the Dunkers. Imitation played a part also in their insistence on a trine immersion as the only valid form of baptism, and again in the insistence of all Baptists on immersion. But it was a secondary, not a primary part. The primary impulse that they obeyed was the consciousness of kind, itself the result of heterogeneity in the social composition.

Conditions of life similar to those that surrounded the Christians of the early church surrounded them. It was the poor that were involved in the movement. They had little hope for better things in this world. No more than the early Christians did they share in the government.

On the contrary the government oppressed them. The ascendant religions persecuted them. The doctrines, held by those who persecuted, that had any relation to the oppressions and persecutions, must in the eyes of the persecuted be wrong, especially, when the Scriptures

---

*See American Journal of Theology, Jan. 1905, where a letter of Grebel, one of the leaders of the Baptist party at Zurich, is translated, which sets forth this consciousness of a difference.

were against the contentions of the persecutors. Such were the stimuli that awakened in the Dunkers a consciousness of kind, and influenced them to imitate the doctrines and practices of those to whom they felt themselves socially akin.

Likewise, conscious unlikeness to the members of the state churches is at the bottom of the Dunkers' doctrine of *the Lord's Supper*. The first thing that excited their opposition to the rite as observed in the tolerated churches was the fact that people of the sort they described as "unregenerate" were admitted to the Lord's table.

Whether such people were not good is beside the question. They were different from the Dunkers socially, i. e., they were of a different social class from that to which Mack and his friends belonged, and therefore did not live the kind of life that the Dunkers thought they should live in order to be recipients of the Lord's Supper. That fact led to an interpretation of their conduct that unfitted them in the eyes of the Dunkers for participation in so sacred a rite.

Furthermore, when criticism of the rite had once begun, it was easy to proceed with it further. Consciousness of kind suggested imitation of the primitive Christians in the observance of the rite. That is shown by the assertion repeated even to tiresomeness by the Dunkers, that they are the true followers of the primitive Christians. This imitation gave rise to the positive elements in the Dunkers' doctrine of the Lord's Supper. The New Testament, as the organic law of their new society, suggested a full meal eaten in the evening. This was confirmed by the history of the rite in the early church.

This feeling of likeness to the primitive Christians also led to the adoption of *the rite of Feet Washing* according to the practice of the Apostles recorded in Jno. 13.

The commandment of Jesus there, confirmed them in their position.

Their *doctrine of the state* was an outgrowth of the same sort of reasoning. The government had made itself obnoxious to them. On matters which they felt should, on Protestant principles, be left to the individual conscience, it persecuted them. It was identified with every social institution against which they revolted with all the strength of their moral natures.

The reason of the Dunkers' *refusal to bear arms*, and *to take oaths* lay in a similar opposition to a government that oppressed them, as that which provoked resistance by the early Christians to war and the use of the oath, and also by the Jews in the period preceding the advent of Christ.* They were keenly conscious of a difference between themselves and the governing class and all persons that were connected with the latter.† Feeling themselves right before God, they necessarily regarded as wrong those beliefs and practices of their enemies, which were in any way responsible for the harsh conduct of the latter towards them. What, then, could be more wrong than the state and the clergy, the very instruments of their oppression? War must be wrong, because it was the instrument by which innocent and good men were made to suffer.

The oath must be wrong, because it was the sacred instrument of the state, and the state abused the righteous; because it was used by men that hated the just; because it was an instrument of evil consecrated by a religious sanction. Scripture, of course, became a weapon of defence. Of all the Anabaptists only those of Muenster believed in war. They held to it because of their doctrine

---

*See Charles, "Slavonic Enoch" 49: 1, 2.

†Spener, who never left the Lutheran church, although the leader of the Pietists, believed war God-ordained. See his "Bedencken", 1: 14.

of the present millennial kingdom of Christ on earth.

Thus, it is clear that the ideals of the Dunkers arose out of their recognition of the differences between themselves and their more numerous and more powerful, but less pious, opponents. The recognition of these differences grew out of conflicts, which were due to differences in mental and moral characteristics. These, in turn, originated in the diversity of social classes, which, again, was due to a mixture of population. But, again, the heterogeneity of social composition resulted from the physical nature of the country. Therefore, the ultimate cause of the social phenomena that gave rise to the doctrines of the Dunkers was the peculiar physical nature of that part of Germany in which the sect originated. Had it been a secluded region, into which various kinds of people could not go, and where perforce the population must have become homogeneous, the sects of German religious history could not have risen there. Religious differences are due, in the last analysis, to social differences.

CHAPTER III.

The Dunker Organization: Its Origin.

Two circumstances suggested to Mack, his ideal of the church viz., that his doctrines demanded an organ of concrete expression and that the existing churches were hostile to him and his doctrines.

From the conflict of opinions there had emerged the doctrines already described. They related to life, organization and conduct, not to pure thought. Therefore, to exist simply as doctrines would not do; they must have concrete means of expression. Hence, the doctrines demanded a social organization for their realization, and thus gave rise to a positive ideal of society. Here Mack differed from such of his fellow Pietists as Hochmann.

The circumstance, however, that the existing social organizations were hostile to such ideals, and that conflict with such organizations had suggested the doctrines, demanded the creation of a society to give expression to the Dunker ideals. Thus originated the ideal of a social organization that was not hostile to the Dunker doctrines.

Furthermore, the two circumstances named determined the nature of the social organization. The former conditioned the form of the society, in that it must be such that it was fitted to realize the ideals that had risen in opposition to those of the orthodox Churches. The latter determined that it must be different from the organizations with which the Dunkers had come into conflict. Naturally it would differ from these organizations on the points in dispute. Therefore, its conditions of membership, its rites, its ministry and its method of organization must be different. This gave the new society, as well as its doctrines, a decidedly negative tendency. Its laws were stringent, but were negative. Its character was stern. It was severely protestant.

It was said above that the ideal was suggested by conflict. A more detailed description of the social and
physical conditions that existed in the region where the
organization originated will show us the cause of the
conflict.

The physical features of southwestern Germany are
such as to favor great complexity of population. It is a
somewhat mountainous country, yet it is not so rough
that it forbids easy access through its valleys to all its
parts. The Rhine valley furnishes a great natural
channel for currents of migration both from Switzerland
on the south and from all the countries lying to the north,
contiguous to the Rhine. Its natural fertility attracted
a comparatively dense population. It had long been the
mixing ground for the peoples of Western Europe. Wave
after wave of migration had swept over it. The result
was a very composite population. This complexity of
social composition was partly ethnic, but at the close of
the seventeenth century it was more largely political and
social.

These physical features made it inevitable that it
should have classes of conqueror and conquered, feudal
lord and serf, priest and layman, since sufficient time
had not elapsed to enable the governing classes to unify
the population completely.

The broken character of the country, however, also
provided secluded districts in close proximity to each
other. A mountain or a river formed a barrier to
frequent communication in the days before modern means
of travel had over-come these obstacles to social intercourse. This developed diversity of population in the
country as a whole, while it determined that such secluded
regions should become homogeneous. Furthermore,
these physical features determined the small political

divisions in the period between the break down of feudalism and the modern period of German unification. They
had much to do also with the heterogeneity of mental type
and disposition in Germany as a whole that accounts for
the turmoil and strife, both political and religious,
characteristic of the Reformation and Post-Reformation
periods.

The physical environment had determined that the
composition of the population of Wittgenstein, the district
where the Dunkers originated, should be less complex
than in some other parts of this valley. Goebel describes
the region as rough, stony and unfruitful.* It is also a
district isolated somewhat by mountains. These two
facts served to repel rather than to attract outsiders to
its confines. Its unproductiveness and its isolation,
moreover, had effected a lessening of the distance between its rulers and their subjects. In the first place,
because it was a poor country, it happened that, the
rulers did not have the splendor that would have separated
them from their poorer subjects. In the next place,
isolation prevented the emulation of rulers with a more
splendid court, and gave time the opportunity to mould
the rulers and ruled into a social unity. Its meager
economic advantages and its isolation hindered any
considerable immigration, so that the population was
largely autogenous in its origin. These circumstances
conditioned a homogeneity in the subject population
itself.

This homogeneity of the population in Wittgenstein
explains the religious toleration that was the policy of
that country at the beginning of the eighteenth century,
and that made it a place of refuge for the persecuted in

*"Geschichte d. Christlichen Lebens", 2:739.

other places.*   For toleration of any sort is possible
only when the elements of the population have been
assimilated to an ideal more or less common to them
all, or when the population is autogenous in its origin.   In either case the population becomes homogeneous.   Religious toleration is dependent on social homogeneity, since religion is only one of the ideals a
like response to which results in assimilation.

The religious toleration of Wittgenstein and the intolerance of adjacent districts were stimuli a like response
to which brought together at Berleberg and Schwarzenau,
some five or six hundred persecuted Pietists, Separatists,
Enthusiasts and Mennonites.†

After these people from different regions had assembled in Wittgenstein, they found themselves in an entirely new environment.   Secondary stimuli that they had
not yet encountered, began to work upon them.   These
stimuli consisted of the ideals, programmes of reform,
doctrines, and methods of the various leaders in the respective places from which the leaders had come, but
which had not operated upon those in other places, because of the distance by which they were separated and
lack of communication.   Proximity now brought these
various stimuli into the environment of all those settled
in Wittgenstein.

These refugees from persecution in other parts introduced alien elements into the population of Wittgenstein.
While on general pietistic principles and social position
they were one with the population of Wittgenstein, on
minor religious points they differed from it, and those

*Besides Wittgenstein, Prussia and the Netherlands were the only
countries on the Continent where there was religious toleration at this
time.

†Goebel, "Geschichte d. Christlichen Lebens," 2:774.

from each place differed from the emigrants from every
other region. This circumstance led to processes of conflict and selection. Men's responses to these diverse
stimuli were unlike and unequal. Some were prepared
to respond to a stimulus favorably, others adversely.
These responses gave rise to the parties in Wittgenstein.
The unequal responses marked out the leaders and the
followers. Those that responded most heartily became
leaders fully possessed by the ideal to which they responded favorably. Those that responded less heartily
became the followers.

In this environment by a process of selection, Alexander Mack became possessed of a definite programme for
the organization of a Christian society differentiated from
all those with which he was acquainted. This was partly
the result of his reaction upon his experiences as a Pietist, partly of his response to the ideals presented by
Hochmann and others of his friends at Schwarzenau,
partly of his favorable response to the stimuli presented
by the writings of Arnold and Felbinger, and partly the
result of his experiences with the orthodox churches.
Once formulated, this ideal was presented by Mack to his
friends in Schwarzenau. This then became a stimulus
to which they had to respond in some way. Here again
conflict and selection determined the original members of
the Dunker church.

It was under the conditions just sketched and by the
processes described that the Dunkers took their beginning in 1708 at Schwarzenau, in Wittgenstein, within what
was later known as the Grand Duchy of Hesse-Darmstadt.

While the Dunker church has always refused to acknowledge any man as its founder, yet it looks back to
Alexander Mack as the one who had the most to do with
its formation. He was the natural leader of the original

band, and during his life-time was the most influential
person among them both in Europe and, later, in America.   The Dunker writers of later times speak of Mack as
"their teacher," and as "one of their number who was a
leader and speaker of the word in their meetings."*
Mack, born in 1679, and brought up in the Reformed
church, was, when we first hear of him, a wealthy miller
at Schriesheim an-der-Bergstrasse.   This was probably
his birth-place.   Before 1708 he had left Schriesheim,
and had gone to live at Schwarzenau, because of persecution incident to his interest in Pietism and Separatism,† as appears from his son's words in the Introduction to "A Plain View of the Rites and Ordinances, etc." ‡

Aside from this account and a few words in the opening
chapter of the "Chronicon Ephratense," we have no
knowledge of the life of Mack until he went to Schwarzenau.   Here he became acquainted with other Pietists

---

* "Chronicon Ephratense," Eng. trans., p. 1; Mack, "A Plain View, etc."
quoted in Brumbaugh, "History of the Brethren," p. 38, 39.

† I use the word Separatism, not as the designation of any sect, but simply as a term that indicates a very wide-spread tendency of the times.

‡ "It pleased God in his mercy, early in the beginning of this century to
support his 'grace that bringeth salvation, and which hath appeared to all
men,' by many a voice calling them to awake and repent, so that thereby
many were aroused from the sleep and death of sin.   These began to look
around for the truth and righteousness, as they are in Jesus, but they had
soon to see with sorrowful eyes the great decay (of true Christianity) almost in every place.   From this lamentable state of things they were pressed to deliver many a faithful testimony of truth, and here and there private
meetings were established besides the public church organization, in which
newly awakened souls sought their edification.   Upon this the hearts of
the rulers were embittered by an envious priesthood, and persecutions
were commenced in various places, as in Switzerland, Wuertemberg, the
Palatinate, Hesse and other places.   To those persecuted and exiled persons the Lord pointed out a place of refuge, or a little 'Pella,' in the land of
Wittgenstein, where at that time ruled a mild count, and where some pious
countesses dwelt.   Here liberty of conscience was granted at Schwarzenau,
which is within a few miles of Berleberg."—Brumbaugh, *op. cit.*

and separatists that had been driven thither by the persecutions in neighboring districts, the most noted of whom was Hochmann, whose beliefs were noticed in the previous chapter.

It was in a district where the doctrines of such people were received by the rulers, as well as by the people, that Mack lived for some time previous to 1708. From all parts of the country around, men and women of similar opinions had come into Wittgenstein. * Here was a country where all kinds of sectarians were protected in their opinions. What Mack's opinions had been before this we do not know in detail, but from the account, quoted above, it is probable that he had held opinions at Schriesheim that made him the object of persecution there. If so, his removal to Schwarzenau was a step that would tend naturally to accentuate his separatistic proclivities.

As the companion of Hochmann, Mack had the opportunity of visiting many different communities of Baptists (Taufgesinnten) in Germany. † In this way he became acquainted with the various views held by different communities of these sectarians. This experience not only confirmed him in his separatism, but the enforced comparison of the doctrines with which he met led him to an independent study of the subjects that were under discussion, and the formation of idiosyncratic opinions. ‡

After studying the matter for some time he found himself unable to be satisfied with the moderate position of Hochmann on some points of organization. With the latter he was agreed as to the necessity of an internal (mystical) life corresponding to the outward profession, as to

* Goebel, 2: 759 f.

† Mack's "A Plain View," quoted in Brumbaugh, "History of the Brethren", p. 39.

‡ Ibid, p. 36 f.

baptism being only for adults, the office of the Holy Spirit in the selection and qualification of ministers, the function of governments, the Lord's Supper being only for the regenerate, Christian perfection, final restoration of the lost, and as to the low estate of matrimony compared with celibacy.*

But Mack was not content with these positions. He had come under the influence, not only of Hochmann, but also of Gottfried Arnold.† The latter had been professor of Church History at Giessen, 1697-1698. He was a most pronounced separatist, and wrote voluminously on the life in the early Christian churches, with a view to showing that the churches of his times had departed widely from the life and organization of the church of the early centuries of Christianity. He did more than any other one to develop and apply the doctrine then held, at least in theory, by all theologians of the Protestant churches, that true Christianity is Bible-Christianity, and that the early church is its best interpreter.‡

These two men had a most profound influence on Mack's course. But Mack reacted upon them and reached a position independent of them both. He was satisfied neither with the mystical, unorganized separatism of Hochmann, nor with the negative criticism of Arnold. He wished to see embodied in an organized community the elements of truth that he recognized in both. This embodiment, the unorganized Pietists gathered together from all parts of Germany and Switzerland to Wittgen-

*See Chapter II, also Mack's "A Plain View, etc.", quoted in Holsinger, "History of the Tunkers", p 113 f.

†Ibid, p. 77. Jeremias Felbinger's influence on Mack accounts for some doctrines. See "A Plain View, etc.", Holsinger, p 81.

‡See his "Erste Liebe," and "Unpartaische Kirchen-und-Ketzer Historien", *passim.*

stein, and who consisted of men of all shades of opinion, did not afford. *

In the conflict of ideals, therefore, which presented themselves to Mack, there arose in his mind the ideal of a Christian society that was different from that of the orthodox church, on the one hand, and, on the other hand, from the ideal of the church as a mystical, unorganized fellowship based on the recognition of certain Pietistic teachings concerning conduct, held by Hochmann and his friends. This ideal was that of a society based upon the New Testament, interpreted in the light of the history of the primitive church, as its organic and statute law, with a definite organization.

Consequently Mack set about assemblying those who held like opinions with a view to their organization into a community in which these desirable objects could be attained. Finally, in 1708 "eight persons consented together to enter into a covenant of a good conscience with God, to take up all the commandments of Jesus Christ as an easy yoke, and thus to follow the Lord Jesus, their good and faithful shepherd, in joy and sorrow, as his true sheep, even unto a blessed end", to quote the

---

*"Those who were brought together there from the persecutions, though they were distinguished by different opinions, and also differed in manners and customs, were still, at first, all called Pietists, and they among themselves called each other brother. But very soon it appeared that the words of Christ, Matthew 18, where he says, 'If thy brother shall trespass against thee, go and tell him his fault between thee and him alone, etc.'", could not be reduced to a proper Christian practice, because there was no regular order yet established in the church. Therefore some returned again to the religious denominations from which they had come out, because they would not be subject to a more strict Christian discipline; and to others it appeared that the spiritual liberty was carried too far, which was thought to be more dangerous than the religious organizations they had left".—Mack, "A Plain View, etc.", quoted in Brumbaugh, "History of the Brethren", p 36.

quaint description written by Mack's son. * There were
five men and three women.   Two were from Hesse-Cassel,
two, or three, from Schriesheim, one or two from Basle,
Switzerland, and two from Bareit, Wuertemberg.† After
they had come to an agreement as to the necessity of
forming a church, they decided to be rebaptized, because
baptism is the door into the church.   They believed that
they had not been members of the true church of Christ
hitherto, since it had not yet been organized, and since
they had not received the baptism that they believed was
the only Christian baptism.   Therefore, as the first step
to be taken in their new venture, they requested Mack to
baptize them "according to the example of the primitive
and best Christians, upon their faith".‡   But Mack did
not consider himself baptized, and therefore could not
baptize others.   In the difficulty they decided to fast and
pray that they might have the guidance of Christ himself in the matter.   Mack believed in a kind of Apostolic
Succession, but it was not one that was dependent on
men's hands.   Therefore the following expedient was
adopted as the direction of Christ.   They cast lots to
determine who should baptize Mack.   He, in turn, baptized the others.   This satisfied their determination to
be "baptized by the church of Christ", for they consider-

*Brumbaugh, "History of the Brethren", p 37.   Brumbaugh thinks
that a part of this Introduction was an original document printed at
Schwarzenau, but I have seen no evidence for such a conclusion. See Brumbaugh, p 43 n.

†The exact names and former residence of these first eight members it
is not possible to determine.   Ecclesiastically, two had been Lutherans and
the other six members of the Reformed church.   The striking fact, to
which Ritschl has called attention in his "Geschichte d. Pietismus", that
the Reformed church was much more prolific of sects than the Lutheran,
is exemplified by the composition of the membership of the first body of
this denomination.   See Brumbaugh, p. 30.

‡Mack, "A Plain View, etc.", Brumbaugh, p 39.

ed this person designated by the Holy Spirit himself. The name of the person upon whom the lot fell, by common agreement, always remained a secret.

This first baptism occurred in the solitude of the early morning, in the Eder river, a small stream that flows past Schwarzenau, sometime in the year 1708. * After they had come up out of the water, and had changed their clothing, the old record tells us that "they were made at the same time to rejoice with great inward joyfulness, and by grace they were deeply impressed with these significant words. 'Be ye fruitful and multiply'".

Thus, Mack's ideal of a social organization originated as follows:

1. The doctrines suggested by a consciousness of unlikeness to the orthodox Christians demanded a means for their realization.

2. What kind of an organization it should be was determined by this same consciousness of kind. It was an ideal that originated in opposition, on the one hand, to that realized in the organizations already in existence, both orthodox and sectarian. On the other hand, it was an ideal the character of which was determined by opposition to the non-ecclesiastical, mystical ideal of fellowship advocated by Hochmann.

Like the doctrines, Mack's ideal of a social organization was born of conflict. The elements of which it was made up were selected out of a multitude that the social and religious conditions of the time suggested. In large measure, they were selected by Mack because they expressed the opposition he felt to the social organizations representing elements of the population unlike that to

* Mack, "A Plain View, etc"., in Brumbaugh's "History of the Brethren", p 40. We have three lists of names, one of which differs from the other two. See Brumbaugh, p 30.

which he belonged. In short, the ideal of an organization, realized in the Dunker church, was produced by a heterogeneity in the population, which in turn, was conditioned by the natue of the environment.

Thus was inaugurated the sect that came to be known as "Taufers," or "Tunkers," because of their mode of baptism, but who at first called themselves simply "Brethren." Insignificant as that beginning may have seemed to the superficial observer of the time, it was the origin of a religious body which, together with others like it, has had great influence upon American social and political life in certain states of the Union, and that today is contributing not a little to the solid citizenship, and to the national prosperity, and something to the culture of our country. To the student of the social condition of Germany at that time it is interesting for the light it throws on the quality of German religious thought, and on the character of the German people of the lower classes of that period, and, most important of all, from our standpoint, it gives one an interesting glimpse into the processes by which human societies originate, and according to which they develop.

CHAPTER IV.

THE DEVELOPMENT AND CLOSE OF THE MOVEMENT IN EUROPE.

Whenever a number of persons have deliberately come to the same conclusion on a doctrine or an ideal, and on the basis of that similarity have united in association for a common purpose, their zeal for the accomplishment of that purpose varies directly with the development of the consciousness of kind. That is to say, their zeal will be great or small, on the one hand, according as they are conscious of their likeness to each other, and, on the other, according as they recognize their unlikeness to their opponents.

This principle explains the growth of the Schwarzenau congregation and the origin of other Dunker churches. The organization had now been formed at Schwarzenau. It was small, being composed of but eight people. But these were all united in purpose. Discussion of the different doctrines had selected them from the mass of Pietists at Schwarzenau, and had made real their potential similarity. Only those had entered the organization as charter members who were thoroughly convinced of the truth of the positions held by Mack.

A consciousness of likeness among the members of an association, however, is sharpened by the conciouness that, as a group, they are different from other groups in the population. The intensity of their zeal is dependent on this consideration also, for, if they did not feel that they were different from other groups, they would not experience a desire to bring others to their own way of thinking. Thus, consciousness of kind develops zealous activity.

Continued like response to these two classes of stimuli

helped to make perfect the consciousness of kind which
membership in the same social class, like response to
persecution by the tolerated religions, and a more or less
extended period of acquaintance at Schwarzenau had gen-
erated among the first Dunkers. Therefore, to begin
with, Mack had a church composed of members who
were of one mind on the doctrines held and on the purpose of the organization. With a united organization and
a definite program it was possible for the Dunkers to
make a very deep impression on the other Pietists at
Schwarzenau. Consequently, the growth of the church
there, for a time, was very rapid.

However, the manifestation of zeal results in a further
development of likemindedness.* Cause and effect
change places. As consciousness of likeness among the
members of a society increases, the consciousness of likeness among the social groups in a population decreases,
unless, indeed, the population, as a whole, is rapidly becoming unified. Hence, after a period of success among
the population at Wittgenstein, the activity and success
of the Dunkers raised up opposition. Naturally, it took
the shape of discussion, since Wittgenstein did not allow
persecution. Gruber's Questions and Mack's Answers
thereto are the evidences. †

There are two ways in which a society multiplies its
congregations, (1) by missionary preaching, and (2) by
colonization. The first method arises when the surplus
energy of the congregation has no promising field for its
exercise in its own vicinity. This condition may come
about by the absorption of all likeminded persons in the
vicinity, or by the growth of an active opposition, or
both. It arises according to the law of least effort. The
energy seeks the line of least resistance. The second

* See Ross, "Foundations of Sociology," p 96.

† See Mack's "A Plain View, etc.", p. 72 f.

may arise because of persecution in times when that is the mode of expressing consciousness of unlikeness, or, from response to economic opportunities, or, rarely from a like response to opportunities of social service.

At first the zeal of the Dunkers had a field for its expression among the inhabitants of Wittgenstein. But after a time, probably according to the law of rhythm, their success in winning adherents lessened. The zeal of the Dunkers, obeying the law of least effort, then led them to seek converts in other parts of the country. Naturally, Mack went, or sent men, to the people with whom he had become acquainted on his journeys with Hockmann. There converts were made.

These principles enable us to understand the facts of the early history of the Dunkers. Mack and his companions had felt deeply impressed with the necessity of obedience to the command of God to Noah, "Be ye fruitful and multiply". *

Accordingly they threw themselves earnestly into the work of spreading their beliefs. So successful were they that within the first seven years of their history, as an organization, they had not only gathered a considerable congregation at Schwarzenau, "but here and there in the Palatinate there were lovers of the truth, and especially was this the case at Marienborn, where a church was gathered."† There are four places which, we hear, contained members of the Dunker faith. They are Schwarzenau, Crefeld, Marienborn and Ebstein. Besides these places we are told that there were scattered members here and there in the Palatinate, and a few in Switzerland.‡ This seems to have been the widest extent of the Dunker

* Ibid, p. x.

†"A Plain View, etc.", p xi.

‡Ibid, p xi; cf. "Chronicon Ephratense", p 247.

movement in Europe, and this lasted only a comparatively short time.

Such zeal demanded a response. If the population to
which the appeal is made is homogeneous and there is
mental and moral resemblance between it and those
that come as missionaries, as was largely the case at
Schwarzenau, the response is favorable. In case, however, the population of the place to which the missionaries
go is heterogeneous and there is but slight consciousness of likeness between the majority of the people and
those that present an ideal, then the response of this
part of the people naturally will be hostile. This latter
condition prevailed in general at that time in southwestern Germany and Switzerland. The population was composite. The majority of the people were not like Mack
and his fellow-missionaries in mental and practical re-
semblances. Hence, they did not respond favorably to
the ideals the Dunkers presented. Therefore, as well as
converts, the Dunkers also made enemies, who stirred up
persecution against the Dunker converts. As a result of
the persecution the members in Switzerland and the Palatinate had to flee. A part of them removed to Marienborn. These immigrants together with some from other
places constituted the church at that place.

In most cases it is probable, however, that the stimulus
of economic opportunity played some part in the determination of the points at which other congregations should
be established. It was difficult for such large numbers
of people to make a living at Schwarzenau. Therefore,
after the common fund was exhausted, some of them
were forced to seek other places in which to live. Some
went to Marienborn and some to Ebstein and together
with refugees from Switzerland and the Palatinate, formed the original members of churches in those towns.

As soon as these people settled in a place, they felt it incumbent upon themselves to bear witness to their faith. This testimony became a stimulus to which the people and the rulers perforce responded. Some responded favorably, some unfavorably. Persecution originated in the unfavorable responses, and where the Dunkers were not protected by a policy of toleration, it drove them out. That happened to be the case at Marienborn, where persecution closed the history of the Dunker congregation. Some of them went back to Schwarzenau, and some to Crefeld.

What became of the members at Ebstein we can only conjecture. Two of the Dunker ministers in Europe, Christian Libe and Abraham Dubois were from Ebstein. The former went to Crefeld, the latter to Schwarzenau. From this it is possible to suppose that the members of the congregation at Ebstein went to one of the two places just named.* What occasioned the break up of the congregation at Ebstein we do not know. Thus, in 1715 there were but two congregations of Dunkers in Europe, one at Schwarzenau and one at Crefeld.†

We turn now to interpret in some detail the history of

*"A Plain View, etc." p xi.

†It is scarcely possible to infer from the places spoken of in the list of ministers of the Dunker church previous to 1715, given in the Introduction to "A Plain View, etc.," that there were members in other places. During the time from the organization of the church to 1715, the following men were called to the office of the ministry: John Henry Kalkleser from Frankenthal; Christian Libe and Abraham Dubois from Ebstein; John Nass from Norten; Peter Becker from Dillsheim; John Henry Trout and his brothers, Heinrich Holzapple and Stephen Kock, of whose native places we are not told; George B. Ganz from Umstatt; and Michael Echerlin from Strasburg. All of these became ministers at Crefeld, except Kalkleser, Dubois, Ganz and Echerlin, who were at Schwarzenau. Of other members in the places named we know nothing. If there were others besides these ministers they must have removed, or were too few to form a congregation, for we hear of no churches in those places.

these two congregations, Schwarzenau and Crefeld.

The origin of the first of these has been noticed in Chapter II. Of the subsequent history of this congregation down to 1713 we know very little. Located in a land where there was religious toleration it enjoyed apparently an undisturbed prosperity. It is probable that the large numbers of people that had gathered in Wittgenstein from various parts of the country, fleeing thither from persecution, united with the Dunkers. Goebel has a remark that doubtless refers to this. He says, quoting Count Carl Gustavus, that at Schwarzenau (and Elsoff) there were over three hundred families gathered, and in Berleberg (especially in Homrighausen) there were about as many families. Many of these had allowed themselves to be baptized in the Eder by immersion in 1709.* As the Dunkers were the only immersionists in the region, so far as we know, this probably refers to them.

In this congregation during the period before 1713 two interesting features appeared, communism and celibacy. Sometime during this period of the history of this congregation Alexander Mack, the originator of the movement, put his property into the common fund of the congregation. The quaint description of this transaction is found in the "Chronicon Ephratense", the history of the Community at Ephrata, Pennsylvania, founded by Conrad Beissel. It says, "The Schwarzenau Baptists arose in the year 1708; and the persons who at that time broke the ice, amid much opposition, were Alexander Mack, their teacher, a wealthy miller of Schriesheim-an-der-Bergstrasse, who devoted all his earthly possessions to the common good, and thereby became so poor that at last he had not bread enough to last from one day to the

---

*Goebel, "Geschichte d. Christlichen Lebens", 2:774.

next, etc.''* This throws an interesting light on
the internal arrangements of the congregation. This
author asserts that the congregation at Schwarzenau
practiced a kind of communism.†

These same writings also give evidence that in the
early history of the congregation at Schwarzenau celibacy
was the rule. That this practice continued for seven
years, and was then given up is all that we know about
it.

Just what caused this congregation to give up these
features we are not told. In 1713, however, Mack ex-
cuses the Dunkers for having practised them thus:
"That we, however, after baptism had difficulties to
overcome concerning marriage, labor and many other
points, is true; for before our baptism, while we were
yet among the Pietists, we were not otherwise taught by
those who were deemed as great saints. Hence we had
much contention until we gave up our imbibed errors."‡
It is probable, however, that social changes were primary
among the influences that led to their abandonment.
The social unrest that had characterized the period following the influx into Wittgenstein of the diverse social
elements, when the persecuted of other regions fled
thither for protection, had gradually given place to

* "Chronicon Ephratense", p 1. Eng. trans.

†This has been denied by some later Dunker writers. For example,
the author of the Memoir of Alexander Mack, probably James Quinter,
judging from the initials,—J. Q., which are prefixed to the English translation of Mack's "A Plain View, etc", says that Mack lost all his money by
paying fines for the members of his congregation. Part of it doubtless
went in this way, but it is probable that the most of it was used in the
common expenses of the congregation. See "Chronicon Ephratense", p 2
and Gruber's Query 37 with Mack's Answers to it in "A Plain View, etc.,"
p 87.

‡Mack, "A Plain View, etc.," Question 37, p 87.

social assimilation, and social peace. The enthusiasm born of unsettled social conditions was superceded by the calm deliberation that follows social homogeneity. Fanaticism had yielded to sober thought and action.

All this had come about because the population had gradually become more homogeneous. At first the different elements of the population were in conflict. Ideals, modes of thought, and habits clashed. Gradually, however, as the people became acquainted and came to see good qualities in each other, they developed a resemblance to each other, or, in case this did not occur and the one party was not strong enough to vanquish the other in discussion and social position, conflict made way for toleration. Either result made for more settled conditions of society in Wittgenstein.

Moreover, after a time the immigrants settled down to steady occupations. Peace gave opportunity for prosperity. Economic prosperity is the eternal enemy of fanaticism. There was no further need of a communistic sharing of goods, and on the disappearance of that feature there followed the building up of private property and individual homes. With the death of fanaticism there naturally ensued the giving up of belief in celibacy.

While these experiments had no influence on the history of the church in general, they had significance for the early history of the church in America. In Beissel's community at Ephrata, Pennsylvania, both of these features were very prominent, and the strength of their appeal to some of the Dunkers at Germantown shows that this incident at Schwarzenau had not been forgotten.*

The congregation at Schwarzenau was not disturbed by persecution during this period, but its activity incited at least one of the orthodox opponents of the Dunkers,

*See "Chronicon Ephratense", p 102.

viz., Ludwig Gruber, to combat them by skillfully framed questions, to which the Dunkers were asked to reply. Mack as leader of the congregation answered these questions in writing. His reply was considered by the congregation such an excellent apology for the Dunker beliefs that it was published by the church at Schwarzenau in July, 1713. Sometime later there was published with it a tract called, "A Plain View of the Rites and Ordinances of the House of God, Arranged in the Form of a Conversation between a Father and Son". This set forth more fully the positions of the Dunkers.* Thus the first book of the Dunkers grew out of consciousness of kind.†

The incidents in the history of this congregation from 1713 down to 1720 have left no trace. Evidently it prospered in its religious freedom under the Count of Wittgenstein. But in 1719 on the death of Count Henry of Wittgenstein, the ruler that had protected them in their freedom to worship as they pleased, persecution broke out against them, according to Goebel, and caused them to remove to Friesland and ultimately to America.‡ Whether all the congregation of Dunkers at Schwarzenau left with this party we do not know. The administrator of the Count at Schwarzenau in 1720 could say concerning this only, "that for a long time many pi-

---

*These two tracts are translated by Holsinger in his "History of the Tunkers, etc." p 45 f, together with a translation of the Introduction written by Alexander Mack Jr. in January, 1774. Holsinger called his chapter "Mack's Book." They have been translated and published in pamphlet form by the Brethren's Publishing Company, Mt. Morris, Ill'' 1888.

†Evidently, in the eyes of the separatists of Schwazenau, Mack came out best in the discussion, as most of them joined the Dunkers the next year.

‡Goebel, "Geschichte d. Christlichen Lebens," 2:776.

ous people have lived around here, of whom no one heard any thing bad, but perceived that they conducted themselves in a wholly quiet and pious manner, and by no one had a complaint been made of them. There were about forty families of them, about two hundred persons, that lately have betaken themselves entirely out of the land, of whom it is said that they were Anabaptists (Wiedertaeufer.) The rest of those who yet live about Schwarzenau are Catholics, Lutherans and Reformed in religion. However, whether any of the above-named persons, who are forbidden the Kingdom, stay about here, is unknown to me.''*   Evidently Goebel has given the place of their final destination, not the place to which they went immediately on their leaving Schwarzenau. In 1720 the emigration was not to America, but to Westervain, West Friesland.† This occurred the next year after Peter Becker and his party had left Crefeld for America.

In Friesland the congregation continued its existence under Mack's leadership until 1729, when at least 116 members came with Mack to America in the ship Allen from Rotterdam, *via* Cowes.‡   In the nine years' sojourn in West Friesland some additions were made to the membership.** Thus closed the history of the original congregation of Dunkers in Europe.

The Crefeld congregation had a shorter history. It began in 1715 by the removal thither of the members from other places.

Those that chose Crefeld did so for three reasons, (1)

*Goebel, "Geschichte d. Christlichen Lebens," *op. cit., ibid.*

†Morgan Edwards quoted in Rupp's, "Religious Denominations," p 92 f; See also Brumbaugh, "History of the Brethren," p 45.

‡See the list of these in Brumbaugh, "History of the Brethren" p 54. Also see "Pennsylvania Archives," Second Series, 17:18.

**Brumbaugh, "History of the Brethren", p 54, 93.

because of the situation and economic opportunity, (2) because of religious toleration at Crefeld, (3) because of a consciousness of likeness between themselves and the large number of Mennonites there, a people in most respects like the Dunkers. Not all the members of the congregation at Crefeld were from the original congregation at Schwarzenau. Some were from Marienborn whence they had been driven by persecution, possibly some from Ebstein, while it is probable that many of the members in Switzerland and the Palatinate mentioned by Alexander Mack Jr., went to Crefeld, when persecution drove them from those places. Thus, diverse elements entered into the composition of the Crefeld congregation, a circumstance which throws light upon the checkered history of this church.

This congregation thrived well for a time. It was in a prosperous manufacturing community under the religious freedom granted by the King of Prussia. Moreover, Crefeld was a city in which there had assembled a great many Mennonites that had been driven from Switzerland by persecution.* The latter sect had many points of belief in common with the Dunkers, and, furthermore, it had sympathy for all those that were persecuted for conscience sake. There was in Crefeld much intercommunication between the two sects, Dunkers and Mennonites. Many of the Mennonites joined the Dunkers, just as they did later in Pennsylvania.† On the whole, therefore, this city was a favorable one for the development of a strong Dunker congregation.

But sometime between 1715 and 1719 discord arose, and a division of the congregation occurred. It came

---

*Mueller, "Geschichte d. Bernischen Taeufer", p 194, 228. Also Goebel, "Geschichte d. Christlichen Lebens", 2:846.

†See Brumbaugh, "History of the Brethren", p 51.

about in this way: A young minister in the Dunker church at Crefeld by the name of Hoecker formed an attachment for the daughter of a merchant of Crefeld who was himself a member of the Dunkers, but who had been a Mennonite, and who still preached for the latter for 800 gulden a year. Hoecker was a more scholarly man than most of those in the ministry among the Dunkers at Crefeld, and was very active in the work. This created a jealousy on the part of some of the other ministers against him. The young lady, to whom he finally was married by her father, was not a member of the Dunker congregation. This gave those who were envious of Hoecker an opportunity to express their consciousness of kind. Christian Libe, who had been a very zealous preacher of Dunker views in all parts of the Rhine Valley, and had been imprisoned for two years on the galleys for preaching forbidden doctrines in Basle, together with four other single ministers decided to place the ban upon Hoecker.* It is uncertain whether their reason was that he had married out of the church, or that he, a minster, had married at all, contrary to the teaching of Paul in 1 Cor. 7. The fact that the ministers who decided to put Hoecker under the ban were single men as well as the asceticism of some of the early Dunkers gives color to the latter explanation. On the other hand, the fact that George Adam Martin says that Libe afterwards married out of the congregation contrary to his own principles in the case of Hoecker, and the hostile attitude of the Dunker church from early times down to the present to marriages with anyone outside the Dunker church would tend to sustain the latter hypothesis. However, whatever the reason given, it

*For the details of Libe's imprisonment on the galleys see Muller, "Geschichte d. Bern. Taeufer", p 226 f.

is probable that the real cause of the trouble was a feeling of difference between Hoecker and the others which can be traced back to the diverse social elements that entered into the composition of the membership of this congregation.

John Nass, the elder in charge of the church, and Peter Becker, another minister and the friend of Hoecker were not in favor of excommunicating him. As a compromise they offered to suspend him from participation in the Lord's supper. In this the majority of the congregation agreed. But this mild measure did not satisfy Libe and his partisans. They declared that Hoecker was under the ban, and proceded to treat him as such. In that day this was a very severe punishment, as no member of the church, no matter whether related to him by the closest ties, was to have anything to do with the one under the ban, not even to sit at the same table, or have any conversation with him.*

The two parties could not agree. Potential resemblance did not exist. The longer they discussed the matter, the stronger each side became in its conviction that it was right. The resulting division was what might have been expected under the circumstances. The congregation was made up of people from many different parts of Europe. They had not been subjected to the same environment. In the short time that they had formed a congregation in Crefeld they had not yet had time to become perfectly assimilated. There were two extremes among these separatists that constituted the Dunkers. The one was inclined to be mystical and austere; the other was more moderate in its tendencies.†
Here the two came to an open clash.

*See Mack, "A Plain View, etc.," p 59, 60.

†See Goebel, "Geschichte d. Christlichen Lebens " ·843 f.

This trouble ruined the congregation at Crefeld. At the time of the outbreak John Nass is reported as saying that there were over one hundred persons who contemplated joining the Dunkers, but refused to do so on account of the trouble.* The outcome of it all was that Hoecker took the matter so to heart that he soon died. His death only added fuel to the flames of hate already burning. Peter Becker, the friend of Hoecker, soon afterwards left Crefeld for Pennsylvania. With him went some of the congregation. The seeds of discord were carried along with them and prevented an organization for some time in America.†

How many were in this emigration we are not able to say definitely. Brumbaugh thinks, on the basis of a statement found in Goebel's "Geschichte d. Christlichen Lebens," 2:776, which has been referred to on pages 71 and 72 above, that about two hundred from Wittgenstein (probably from Schwarzenau) went with Becker to America.‡ But it is quite probable that no such number from any place accompanied Becker.** That with Becker there went the larger portion of the congregation at Crefeld, or, at least, the portion of it that was dangerous in the eyes of the orthodox clergy, is shown by the reference to this migration in the *Acta Synod General*, 1719, 21 *ad*

---

*Martin's Letter quoted in "Chronicon Ephratense," p 249.

†"Chronicon Ephratense," p 3, 249.

‡See Brumbaugh, "History of the Brethren," p 49, note (2).

**My reasons for this are as follows: (1) Because Morgan Edwards in his "Materials towards a History of the Baptists," written in 1770, says that there were about twenty persons who came with Becker. (Rupp's "Religious Denominations," p 92.); (2) because the "Chronicon Ephratense" simply says that there were "several," which would hardly be the adjective used, had there been any such number as two hundred; and (3), because it is probable that the passage of Goebel referred to does not have any reference to the emigration under Becker, but to the removal of the Dunkers

44, as follows: "The preachers of the Meuro classe have received the confession of faith of the so-called Dompelaers staying at Creyfelt, and they have sent their 'remonstration' to his gracious Majesty the King of Prussia. However, this *Fratres Meursanae Synodi* report with pleasure that these Dompelaers, who have have been so injurious to our church, have taken themselves away by water and are said to have sailed to Pennsylvania."*

However, some members were left in Crefeld. Over these John Nass and Christian Libe continued to preside. But these two leaders soon fell out. John Nass called Libe a pill-monger in the presence of the congregation, and then withdrew into retirement until he came to America in 1733, leaving Christian Libe in charge of the congregation. The church did not prosper under the leadership of Libe. George Adam Martin reported that, "the Brethren who had been prisoners withdrew, the whole congregation was given up, and everything went to ruin."† Libe became a wine merchant, and married out of the church, in violation of his own rules in regard to Hoecker.

What become of the members that were left at Crefeld it is impossible to say positively. Perhaps some, like John Nass, afterwards went to America. Doubtless, some of the members accompanied Mack to West Fries-

from Schwarzenau to West Friesland in 1719, whence they finally emigrated to America. It would not be at all strange, if they went first to Crefeld, and there picked up some members of the congregation that had remained behind when Becker left with his company for America, and thence went on to West Friesland. This reference in Goebel, on this hypothesis, throws light upon Mack's party, but none whatever upon Becker's. This explanation also has the advantage of resolving the difficulty involved in Brumbaugh's theory.

*Quoted from Brumbaugh, "History of the Brethren," p 51.

†"Chronicon Ephratense", p 248. Why Nass called Libe a pill-monger is not recorded.

land and went with him thence to America. Some, no doubt, joined the Mennonites, or some of the other churches at Crefeld. The real history of this congregation closed in 1719, when Becker and his party left for America.

The difference in the conditions prevailing at Schwarzenau and at Crefeld explains the difference in the history of the two congregations. The physical environment of Crefeld was different from that of Schwarzenau. The former was a flourishing manufacturing town. It had become famous for its linen weaving. It lay in the lower valley of the Rhine much closer to the sea and much less secluded than Schwarzenau. The latter was a place, shut off from the rest of the world, and without the economic advantages of Crefeld.

These differences in the physical environments had made the composition of the Dunker population at Crefeld much more heterogeneous than that at Schwarzenau, because the elements of the congregation at the former place had been assembled from various places by persecution, while the congregation at Schwarzenau had been built up by a process of selection.

Furthermore, before the membership of the Crefeld congregation could be unified by a like response to the Dunker doctrines and ideal of unity for a long period, the conflict of two ideals divided the congregation. This made it impossible for the congregation to present unitedly an ideal to the world, and prevented the pursuit of a policy of unification and consequently the growth of the church there. Consequently it went to pieces.

The physical and geographical situation of Crefeld made it more accessible to influences from England and Holland in the interest of colonization schemes in America, while, on the other hand, the more general consciousness of kind, developed by kindred experiences, caused the Dunkers in Crefeld to respond favorably to the Mennonite and Quaker schemes of colonization. Thus, the physical environment together with other influences determined the presence of the Dunkers at Crefeld, made easy the withdrawal of any dissatisfied members, when the occasion arose, and determined a composite membership in the congregation, and so conflicting ideals.

At Schwarzenau, on the other hand, the congregation was gradually built up out of elements that had many points of similarity and therefore were capable of assimilation by a process of selection in response to the ideals of Mack, instead of by the sudden aggregation of elements socially unlike. A perfect society is not formed by a single like response to stimulus, but by a like response repeated often enough to create an effective like-mindedness. This the twelve years of like response to the ideals of Mack accomplished. This period also enabled Mack to realize his ideal of unity for the congregation. It gave him time to weld it into a homogeneous whole.

In 1719 the political conditions in Wittgenstein changed. The tolerant prince died, and was succeeded by one that had been subjected to different conditions. The policy of religious freedom gave place to one of persecution of all sectarians. A like response to this stimulus took about 200 of the Schwarzenau Dunkers to Crefeld, and thence to West Friesland. At Crefeld some of the congregation that had remained there after the departure of Becker, conscious of their likeness to Mack's party, responded to the invitation of their brethren from Schwarzenau and went along.

Thus, on the whole, Wittgenstein was a political environment that at first sheltered and then became hostile to the sectarians of peasant origin. It was a religious environment that, for a time, was free and then, after the protection of the Counts of Wittgenstein was withdrawn in 1719, it was an unfriendly environment. Hence, the conditions there were such that for a time they attracted people from many parts of the country, and subsequently became such that they forced certain people out.

The removal of this congregation to America was the result of a like response to the stimuli of their enviroment in Friesland, and of their prospective home in the New World, coupled with a like response to the ideals of religous and political liberty presented by the letters of their brethren in America, and the advertisements of land companies, of William Penn and of the sovereigns of England. That some of their comrades in faith followed later instead of going with them was due to the unequal response of the latter.

The members of the congregation at Ebstein and Marienborn now either had been driven by persecution to Crefeld or had been dispersed; the congregation at Crefeld had been divided, and the major portion had removed to America; and the original congregation at Schwarzenau had gone to Friesland, and finally to Pennsylvania. All that remained of the movement in Europe were the broken fragments of the Crefeld congregation, and the few scatterd members throughout the Palatinate and Switzerland, if, indeed, any were left in the latter country. What became of these members is not know. Apparently the movement died out with the removal of these two congregations, for George Adam Martin, sometime after 1757, was able to say without fear of contradiction that "not a branch is left of their Baptist business in all Europe."* The zeal of the few who remained in Europe

*Letter quoted in "Chronicon Ephratense", p 248.

grew cold and they went back to the state churches, or were again drawn into "awakened" circles by such leaders as Count Zinzendorf, who appeared in these districts in 1730. Some few may have crossed the ocean to join their comrades in belief in America in the years that followed the two great Dunker emigrations, 1719 and 1729.* Thus closed the Dunker movement in Europe, to find a more congenial environment in America, to develop from a narrow sect into a respected denomination of useful Christian citizens.

SOCIOLOGICAL SUMMARY.

How many Dunkers there were in Europe we do not know. It is impossible to form an estimate of any value from the number of ministers given by Alexander Mack Jr., for this list is not exhaustive, and the Dunkers did not have one minister to a congregation, as did most of the Christian churches of that time.†

On the basis of what Goebel says as to the number of people that left Schwarzenau for America in 1720, already referred to, it is possible to estimate the number of members at Schwarzenau. But it must be only an estimate, for we do not know whether all the members there emigrated, and we cannot be sure that all of the 200 mentioned were Dunkers.

As to the numbers at Crefeld we are totally in the dark. We know that about twenty came to America with Becker, and it is probable that some of those that went with Mack to West Friesland from Crefeld came with him to America. But how many were left at Crefeld we do not know. The closest approach to an exact figure is that

---

*See letter of John Nass to his son, written from Germantown in 1733; also, Sauer's letter in Brumbaugh, "History of the Brethren," p 108.

†Mack, "A Plain View, etc", p xi.

given by Dr. Brumbaugh in his "History of the Brethren." He has brought together a list of 225 members
that joined the church in Europe. But this list is incomplete, and further investigations may show that ther
were others. More definitely than this it is impossible
at this time to speak. They never had more than four
congregations.*

Characteristic of both congregations was their zeal.
With the abandon generally found in the adherents of
new sects they "were the more powerfully strengthened
in their obedience to the faith they had adopted, and were
enabled to testify publically in their meetings to the
truth", to quote the words of Mack Jr. in his Introduction to "A Plain View". This resulted in the rapid
spread of their faith, but also in the active opposition of
the ministers of the orthodox churches. Hence, they
were called upon to endure persecutions. In these
persecutions the leaders were soon put to the test upon
their doctrine of the non-resistance of evil. That they
stood the test is shown by the record, "There were
those who suffered joyfully the spoiling of their goods,
and others encountered bonds and imprisonment".† On
the whole, the impression that is made on one as he
studies the few remains of this period of their history is
that the members of these first congregations were men
and women of almost terrible earnestness. One can
scarcely appreciate in these days of religious peace how
intense were the religious emotions of those days, when
religion was the one matter of universal interest, and
when for their opinions men were often called upon to
die. The things for which they contended now appear

---

*See names and numbers in the first part of this chapter.

†Mack's Introduction to "A Plain View, etc.", p xi; Cf. "Chronicon
Ephratense" p 1.

trivial, but to them they were vital. Into the discussion of them they threw all their powers of mind. For the defence of them they risked all.

The explanation of this fervor is to be sought in the conflict born of diversity of elements in the population. As these elements became assimilated the conflict was succeeded by toleration, zeal was displaced by calm thoughtfulness, and the willingness to die for one's convictions gave place to calculating consideration of one's own safety and comfort.

Another characteristic of this early period of their history is that the movement was not clearly differentiated in practices, and doctrines from the great body of pie-. tistic separatists of the time. Men's thoughts had not yet become clear and definite as to just what should be done. The relation of the Dunkers to the persecuting churches was clear enough even from the beginning, for it was in opposition to them and their doctrines that the ideals of Mack had come to conscious expression. But the relation of the Dunker organization and doctrines to the other sectarian parties and beliefs of the period at first was rather indefinite, except with regard to the necessity of organization and the emphasis to be given to certain doctrines. Therefore, the opposition to the other sects and the non-ecclesiastical, religious parties was very much less than that felt towards the persecutors, and for this reason the relation of the Dunkers to them much less clear and definite.

Moreover, the consciousness of likeness to many of the sects made for this lack of clear definition of attitude towards them. Hence, some were members, doubtless, who were not fully convinced of all the positions taken by the congregation, but were in general agreement with them, while some, convinced of the truth of the doctrines,

were not members, because of the distance from a Dunker congregation and the impossibility of removal to
Crefeld or Schwarzenau.   This circumstance gives one
the impression, at first glance, that there was no organization at the beginning.   On the contrary, there was an
organization, but naturally it was not as definite in some
respects as it became in time.

As for the organization of the Dunkers, it developed
pari passu with their social experience.   In every case,
consciousness of likeness, or, on the other hand,
of unlikeness to other elements in the population
led to changes in the organization.   In Europe the
organization developed only as far as the opposition to
the orthodox opponents and the unorganized separatists
demanded it.   There is no record that there was any
such thing among them in Europe, for example, as an
Annual Meeting.   As we shall see, that sprang out of the
opposition of the Dunkers to Zinzendorf and his sectarian
allies in Pennsylvania.   The local congregation was the
only organization among the Dunkers in Europe.

Thus, clearness of doctrinal statement, emphasis upon
certain practices and clearly defined attitude towards other organizations and parties came only as a result of conflict
due to consciousness of dissimilarity.   The presence of
unlike elements in the population, and in the congregation gave rise to conflict.

Moreover, the nature of the composition of the membership of the Dunker congregations in Europe determined the attitude of the organization towards the individual.
Thus, in the congregation at Schwarzenau there were
only like elements, and we hear of no coercion of
the individual.   On the other hand, at Crefeld, the
congregation was made up of different elements, and
there a policy of coercion was soon attempted.   The

attempt of Libe to force a policy of uniformity on the congregation in the matter of marriage, illustrated by his attitude towards Hoecker, is a case in point.

Several things conspired to close the history of the Dunker church in Europe:

1. Persecutions made flight from one country to another necessary, and loosened the bonds that bound them to the home country. This also helped to beget the readiness to escape to any country where liberty of conscience was granted.

2. As early as 1682 William Penn had conveyed 5000 acres of land in Pennsylvania to Jacob Tellner of Crefeld. Penn had already in 1677 been on a preaching tour to Germany, and had met many of the people there. Tellner had been in America between 1678 and 1681. Then in 1682 began that enterprise that finally culminated in the organization of the Frankfort Land Company, of which Pastorius was the agent, and of which five of the members were residents of Frankfort, two of Wesel, two of Lubeck, and one of Duisberg. Nearly all of them were Pietists in the general sense of the term. The object of this company was colonization.

In 1683 Penn sold three gentlemen of Crefeld, viz., Remke, Arets and Van Bebber, 1000 acres each. Their aim likewise was colonization. Thus it becomes evident at a glance what forces were set at work among these Crefelders themselves to get people to migrate to Pennsylvania. As a result, in 1683 a colony of thirteen emigrants, of whom at least eleven were from Crefeld, sailed for Pennsylvania, where they founded the city of Germantown.* Most of the members of this colony were Mennonites, but the fact that fellowtownsmen had come to this country, that they wrote back glowing reports of

*See Pennypacker, "Historical and Biographical Sketches," p 13 f.

its advantages, and that they were people with whom the
the Dunkers in Crefeld had much intercourse, made it
very easy for the Dunkers to decide where to go when
once the occasion arose for their removal. The owners
of this land naturally saw to it that the Crefelders did
not lack information and solicitation.

Besides the influence that these two colonization companies exerted to induce emigration, William Penn himself was leaving no stone unturned to bring to the attention of the sturdy Germans, by the plentiful use of printer's ink, the advantages offered by his American province.* In addition to the advertising Pennsylvania received from these private parties, Queen Anne of England
and later George I. sent descriptions of their colonies in
America broadcast throughout these parts of Europe.†
All this publicity not only incited the desire to migrate,
it also gave to desire direction.

3. The general social conditions were bad. The
promise of a better land with greater opportunities
strengthened the appeals of the companies seeking colonists. These facts account for the close of the work
at Crefeld.

4. Once a body of the Dunkers were in America, and
were experiencing liberty and larger economic opportunities, their letters were a most powerful means of induc-
ing those that remained in Europe to go to America.
This accounts for the removal in 1729 of the congregation
that had settled in West Friesland. Most of the mem-

---

*See Sachse, "The Fatherland", in Proceedings of Penna. Ger. Soc., 7:
157 f.

†"Journal of the House of Commons", 16: 597. Rupp in his reference to
this in his "Thirty Thousand Names" has made an error as to the page.

bers of the two congregations in Europe had gone to
America, and the leading spirits among the Dunkers were
there also. Therefore, there was every reason for the
scattered members that remained in Europe either to
migrate thither, or to join some other church. From
1729 on there was a more or less steady stream of Dunkers from Europe to America. John Nass the former elder in charge of the Crefeld congregation went to America
in 1733, and some of his children a few years later.

5. On the other hand, the condition of things in the
congregations themselves had a great deal of influence
upon their later history. Because of the lack of homogeneity in the membership of the church at Crefeld,
trouble arose, which reinforced the appeals of the Crefelders in America to the Dunkers in Crefeld to emigrate
thither.

Environmental conditions had assembled Anabaptist
people at Crefeld and at Schwarzenau. After they united with the Dunkers, a new set of stimuli was brought to
bear. The Dunkers at once began to hold before them
the ideal of unity. This tended to confirm them in their
decision, and further to differentiate them from their
neighbors. But the ideal of unity was held with varying
degrees of earnestness by different members. They had
come together from different parts of the country and
had been exposed to various influences. Thus, Christian
Libe had been subjected to a harsher treatment than
most of the others. He had been banished from Basle,
Switzerland, as an Anabaptist. He had been forced to
work on a galley for two years because of his return
thither to preach his beliefs and to baptize.* This harsh
treatment had engendered an austerity of spirit that

*See "Chronicon Ephratense," p 248; Mueller, "Geschichte d. Bern.
Taeufer," p 226.

heterogeneity in the social composition of the church tended to bring to expression. Dissension produced further differences among those left at Crefeld, as it did also among those that came to America. It prevented the congregation left at Crefeld from presenting its ideals so effectively to those that had not yet united with it. It is only when heterogeneity is on the whole subordinate to a dominant homogeneity that progress without disruption is possible. In Becker's party that went to America homogeneity, though imperfect, prevailed.

With the Schwarzenau congregation the conditions were different. In the first place, the homogeneity of the social group was greater. Then during the twelve years of growth, undisturbed by internal dissension, opportunity was given for Mack to impress his ideal upon the congregation, and thus make the homogeneity yet greater. Finally, persecution, suffered in common, bound the membership more closely together, so that Mack's ideal of unity was realized. Heterogeneity of the population in the region about Schwarzenau accounts for the emigration thence, while the consciousness of their kinship with the Dunkers already in America, coupled with the greater religious and economic opportunities there, explains the emigration of the congregation from Friesland.*

*See Spencer, "First Principles," Sec. 174. Also, Giddings, "Principles of Sociology," p 400 f, and his "Theory of Social Causation," in Publications of the American Economic Assoc., Third Series, Vol. V, Part II.

PART II   THE DUNKERS IN AMERICA

CHAPTER I.

Social Conditions in America Bearing on Population.

The difference between social conditions in Europe and in America created an unstable equilibrium that made movement in the line of least resistance inevitable. We have noticed the condition of society in Europe, which accounts for the emigration of the Dunkers. We must now examine in some detail the conditions in America, which determined where they should go, when they decided to leave Europe. These general social conditions may be classed under three heads, Political, Economic and Religious.

1. Political Conditions in America, with Special Reference to Conditions in Pennsylvania.

The despotism of Europe furnished the occasion, at least, for the foundation of the free American colonies. Almost all the colonies were founded by men and for men who were fleeing from despotism. However, among the colonies there were vast differences in respect to the liberty granted to the inhabitants. For example, the political liberty enjoyed by the middle colonies, especially by Maryland and Pennsylvania, was much greater than was that of most of the New England colonies. This was due to the fact that the charters granted to the proprietors "went farther toward guaranteeing the existence of legislatures within the colonies than did those which created the corporations".*

This democratic tendency was strongest in Pennsylvania. Penn himself was not of royal blood. He belonged by birth to the great middle class. By religion he was associated with a sect that drew most of its recruits, not from the aristocracy, but from the middle and lower classes of society.

Penn identified himself with the colonists to an extent never attempted in any other country or colony.† He never attempted to restrict political rights to the members of his own sect, as political liberty was restricted to members of the dominant sect in Massachusetts, for example. And unlike Carolina and Maryland at certain periods, Pennsylvania was never domineered politically by its proprietor. Further as contrasted with the procedure in Maine and in Carolina, the scheme of government for Penn's Colony was submitted for approval to the colonists. The Council instead of being appointed, was elected. This was an exception to the general rule in the colonies, except in the Carolinas and the Jerseys, where it was an elective body in a qualified way. The acts of this Council the governor had no right to veto. There was, moreover, an elective Assembly, or lower house, which, while it could not originate legislation, could ratify or refuse to ratify measures proposed by the Council.

It should be noticed further that in 1696, in Markham's Frame of Government, the right was given to the Assembly to initiate legislation.‡ In spite of the fact that, when Penn returned in 1700, he declared that the frame

---

*See Osgood, "American Colonies in the 17th Century," 2:74, 254 f.

†Ibid, p 256. Also, Pastorius' Letter, quoted in Pennypacker, "Settlement of Germantown," p 85.

‡Osgood, "American Colonies, etc.," 2:275; Cf. "Colonial Records," 1:48.

of government granted by Markham had been only a temporary expedient during his absence and that the old frame of government of 1683 was again in force, the Council decided to take what was best in both the old frame and Markham's frame and construct a new scheme of government. The result was the Charter of Privileges, passed in 1701, and confirmed by Penn.* By this charter the Assembly was made the only house of legislation, while the Council became an appointive body, without legislative power, but with power to act simply as an advisory board to the governor. Thus at the beginning of the eighteenth century, Pennsylvania, more than any other colony, had placed political power in the hands of the colonists.

It was in Pennsylvania and New Jersey that the establishment of courts was first placed in the hands of the legislature. In most of the other colonies that power was in the hands of the executive.†

While, therefore, in some of the other colonies the procedure was more regular, in Pennsylvania there was a nearer approach to democracy. Political liberty there was of wider extent than elsewhere, both as regards the franchise and also as regards the power of the people's representatives in shaping the government.

Most important of all was the attitude of the proprietor himself to his province. No other proprietor set out with such avowed democratic aims as did Penn. None conceived of his duties in such an ethically paternalistic fashion as he. Consciously Penn had aimed to make for the colony a government that should have primarily as its end, not his own personal power, glory or wealth, but

*"Colonial Records," 2:56 f.

†Osgood, "American Colonies," 2:287.

"the good and benefit of the freeman of the province".*
The Province was his only that he might make the inhabitants of it freer, and give them conditions where they
could live as brothers, and where they could have opportunity to realize their best and highest ideals.   Primarily
not money or power was Penn's aim, but to provide freedom from those conditions, political, economic and religious, that made the Old World a hard place for the common people to live in.   In his own words Penn's Colony
was "a holy experiment".   As such it made a strong appeal to all who were sufferers from despotism in Europe.

2. ECONOMIC CONDITIONS IN PENNSYLVANIA.

In a new and wild land, where industries are in their
infancy, where commerce is undeveloped and money is
scarce, one hardly expects good economic conditions.
In Pennsylvania at the beginning of the eighteenth
century there was little wealth.   But bad as were
the conditions here, they were better than in those parts
of Europe from which the immigrants came.   Money was
worth much more than in Europe.   That is to say, it
would buy more.   On the other hand, the price of land
was low, which was a primary condition of prosperity for
the poor agricultural peasants of Europe.   About 1717 in
Eastern Pennsylvania, where land was considered very
high in price, the agent of George I. quoted it at from 20
to 100 pounds sterling per 100 acres.† Penn offered land
to all who would come at the rate of 100 acres for 40 shillings, or, what Fiske says was equivalent to between $40
and $50, subject only to the quit rent of one shilling per
100 acres per annum.‡   In 1736, 147 acres of land   near

*"Colonial Records of Pennsylvania," 1:58, 63; also "Charter and Laws,"
p 515.

†Quoted in Pennypacker, "Historical and Biographical Sketches," p 187.

‡Fiske, "Dutch and Quaker Colonies," 2:154.

Ephrata, Lancaster county, were sold for 66 pounds, 3 shillings, subject to the usual allowance of 6 per cent. for roads and highways. In 1754 this same parcel of ground sold for 600 pounds.* In 1732, 500 acres, on which Lancaster is now situated, sold for 31 pounds, 10 shillings.† In 1717, Penn's commissioners conveyed 400 acres of land in Springtown Manor, Chester county, for 40 pounds.‡ In 1701, Logan sold for Penn 1000 acres in East Jersey for 300 pounds.** In his prospectus to settlers and adventurers Penn set his price at 100 pounds sterling for each 5000 acres, subject to the quit rent of 1 shilling for each 100 acres per annum. He also offered to give to each master who brought over servants, 50 acres for every servant brought over, when the latter's time had expired, with a quit rent of 2 shillings per annum. To those who could not afford to buy land Penn offered to rent land at the rate of 200 acres, which was the maximum to be rented to any one man, for 1 pence per acre per annum.†† Penn sold to Thomas Woolwich of Stafford, England, on March 22, 1681, 1000 acres for 20 pounds and the quit rent of 1 shilling per annum for each 100 acres, and on July 27, 1681, 500 acres more at the same rate.‡‡ These examples will serve to give us a fairly accurate conception of the prices of land that prevailed in the various periods of German immigration.

The following lists of prices of products at the dates

*Original deeds in possession of the Trustees of the Society of Seventh Day Baptists at Ephrata, Penna.

†Sener, "Lancaster Townstead," in Lancaster County His. Soc., Historical Papers, 5:122.

‡Sener, 'Lancaster Townstead" in Lancaster County His. Soc., Historical Papers, 5:124.

**Memoirs of Penna. His. Soc., 9:68.

††Hazard, "Annals," 1:510, 518, 523.

‡‡Ibid, 1:501.

given are interesting as showing some of the economic
conditions which prevailed in Pennsylvania in those early days:*

1683:

3 Milch Cows with their calves	10 pounds s. d.
Yoke of Oxen	8 "
Brood Mare	5 "
Two Young Sows and Boar	1 ", 10 s
Wheat	3 s 6 d. per bu.
Oats	2 s " "
Barrel of Molasses	1½ pounds.
Beef and Pork	2 d per pound.
Spirits per gal	2 s
Provisions for one yr. for family of five,	16 lbs. 17 s 6d.

1686:

Wheat	3 s, English
money, or 3 s, 6 d, American money	
Pork	2 d per lb.
Beef	3¼ d " "
Wheat	3 s 6 d per bu.
Rye	½ crown " "
Indian Corn	2 s " "

1687:

Pork, per lb.	2½ s.
Butter	6 d.
Rye, per bu.	3 s 8 gro., ¼ cr.
Wheat	3 s or 3 s. 6 d.
Indian Corn	7 groats and 2 s
Lime	6 d.

1690:

Wheat	3 s per bushel.
Barley	2 s " "
Oats	2 s " "
Indian Corn	18 d. " "
Cow and Calf	less than 4 lbs.
Good brood mare	5 pounds.
Beef	12 s per cwt.
Pork	15 s " "
Fat Deer	1¼ s each.

*"Penna. Mag. His. and Biog." 4:447 f.

In Philadelphia, 1766:*

Irish Sheeting..2 s 3 d per yd.
Wide Linen check..2 s 5 d per ell.
Wide Irish Linen...3 s 1 d per yd.
Finer Irish Linen...3 s 9 d " "
Narrow worsted binding for cloths.........................12 s 6 d pr. gro.
Bird eye gartering...1 lb pr. gross.
Women's clocked (?) worsted hose........................1 lb 18 s pr. doz.
Men's grey worsted hose No. 6..............................1 " " " "
    "   "   "   " finer No. 7.........................2 " 4 s " "
Tailor's colored thread ....5 s 6 d per lb.
Pins No. 12..5 s 6 d pr. pkt.
Gross, Sleeve buttons No. 1..................................7 s.
    Ibid   No. 2....................................8 s.
    Ibid   No. 3....................................8 s 12 d
Beaver coating per yd..6 s 1 d
Black trunk..15 s

In 1771 Corn was 4 s per bu., Wheat, 5 s per bu.†

In 1748 the salary of a school teacher was, "A free dwelling in part of the school house, use of part of the school lot, ten cords of wood, half being hickory, and the sum of 10 pounds in silver."‡ Keith's salary in the Friend's School in Philadelphia," was 50 pounds per annum with a house for his family to live in, a school house provided, and the profits of the school besides for one year. For two years more his school was to be made worth 120 pounds per annum."**

These are sufficient to illustrate the opportunities that Pennsylvania offered to agriculturists as compared with the low wages of laborers, and the high prices of land in

*Egle's "Notes and Queries," 3rd Series, 2:108.

†Brumbaugh "His. of Brethren," 284.

‡Quoted in Lancaster His. Papers in "Lancaster His. Soc. Proceedings," 3:100.

**Proud's "Pennsylvania", 1:345. For further contemporary accounts of the economic condition of Pennsylvania at about this time see, Gabriel Thomas', account quoted in Hart's "American History Told by Contemporaries," 2:65-68, and an extract from Richard Castleman's "Voyage, Shipwreck and Miraculous Escape," Ibid, 2:74-77.

the Rhine countries of Germany. From the very district whence came the Schwarzenau Dunkers a traveler so late as 1845 could write, "He (the traveler) will on this excursion observe with pleasure an absence of total destitution in any class of the inhabitants; but that a large portion of the population stands on the verge of great poverty, while a still greater number is involved in privations inseparable from the increase of mouths without a corresponding augmentation of the field of labor, will not escape him. . . . . . Here we shall only remark, that, for want of other occupations, the wages of the laborers are exceedingly low, averaging from 10 d to 1 s per diem for men, and 7 d to 8 d for women. If food be given, 10 kreutzers, or 3½ d is all that is added in money. On the larger farms 4 pounds per annum is the pay of the farm servants, whose board is valued at 5 pounds. From this and the adjacent districts the greatest number of emigrants proceed annually to America. . . . . . A few years back the estimate of the rental of the families of Handshuhshein, according to which they were taxed, averaged 180 florins, or 15 pounds, for each household, as revenue drawn from the land and the occupations that it furnished. We have seen that in this village 378 landowners possessed 1400 Heildelberg morgens: the average was therefore, to each nearly 4 morgens, or something less than 4 English acres."* Compared with such conditions the conditions of life in Pennsylvania were very promising. The immigrants had plenty of land from which they could easily secure a livelihood. If they

---

*T. C. Banfield, "Industry on the Rhine.–Agriculture." p 208 f. This little book is one of the most interesting I have found in giving definite information as to agricultural conditions in Germany. It is, however, a description of conditions at more than a century later than the time of which we are treating, when it might be expected that the heavy emigration of the previous sixty years had made labor scarcer and land more abundant.

could not buy the land, they could rent it. If they had no money to buy tools and with which to begin farming, they could easily find work with others who had.* The necessities of life abounded in plenty by the time the Dunkers arrived.

It must be remembered also that in Europe these peasant folk were not used to much money, and especially during the latter part of their history there they had not been able to get more than the bare necessities of life. For example, many of them did not have money enough to pay their passage way to Pennsylvania.† Numbers of them got over through the assistance of either the Mennonites of Holland or the English Quakers, or by having themselves and their children sold as "Redemptioners" after they got here to pay the ship master for bringing them.‡

More important, perhaps, as stimuli of immigration than the actual economic conditions were the advertisements that Penn caused to be scattered broadcast in Germany, and that later Queen Anne, and King George I., still later, sent throughout the districts of the Rhine countries to induce the persecuted but sturdy Germans to emigrate to America.**

The statement of George I. is the latest of these, and is interesting as showing the very attractive way in which the advantages of America were presented. It was prepared for the special purpose of advertising the lands in west-

*Cf. Pennypacker, "His. and Biog. Sketches," p 185, 188.

†Pennypacker, "Historical and Biographical Sketches" p 190.

‡Nass' letter quoted in Brumbaugh, "History of the Brethren", p 122.

**See "Pennsylvania Magazine of History and Biography", 4:331; also Sachse, "The Fatherland", in Penna. German Soc. Proceedings. 7:162, 175. Rupp in "History of Lancaster County", p 97, 98 quotes Queen Anne's proclamation. Cf. "Journal of the House of Commons", 16:597.

ern Pennsylvania. In this advertisement he contrasts
the conditions in western Pennsylvania with the conditions in Europe and also with the less favorable conditions of eastern Pennsylvania, New York, Virginia and
the Carolinas. He describes the western part of Pennsylvania as a land that has a good climate, pure air
and that offers almost every advantage desired by
immigrants.*

To this glowing description was attached the offer that
each family should have fifty acres of land in fee simple,

*He says that "it is well-watered, having streams, brooks and springs,
and the soil has the reputation of being better than any that can be found
in Pennsylvania and Virginia. Walnut, chestnut, oak and mulberry trees
grow naturally in great profusion, as well as many fruit-bearing trees, and
the wild white and purple grapes in the woods are larger and better than
in any other place in America. The soil is favorable for wheat, barley,
rye, Indian corn, hemp, flax, and also silk, besides producing many other
things much more abundantly than in *Germany.* A field can be planted
for from ten to twenty successive years without manure. It is also very
suitable for such fruit as apples, pears, cherries, prunes, quinces and especially peaches, which grow unusually well and bear fruit in three years
from the planting of the stone. All garden crops do very well, and vine-
yards can be made, since the wild grapes are good and would be still better if they were dressed and pruned. Many horses, cattle and sheep can
be raised and kept, since an excellent grass grows exuberantly. Numbers
of hogs can be fattened on the wild fruits in the bushes. This land is also
full of cattle ·(rundvee), called buffaloes and elks, none of which are seen
in Pennsylvania, Virginia or Carolina. Twenty or thirty of these buffaloes are found together. There are also many bears, which hurt no one.
They feed upon leaves and wild fruits, on which they get very fat, and
their flesh is excellent. Deer exist in great numbers, besides Indian cocks
and hens (turkeys), which weigh from twenty to thirty pounds each, wild
pigeons, more than in any other place in the world, partridges, pheasants,
wild swans and geese, all kinds of ducks, and many other small fowls and
animals; so that if the settlers can only supply themselves for the first year
with bread, some cows for milk and butter, and vegetables, such as pota-
toes, peas, beans, etc., they can find flesh enough to eat from the many wild
animals and birds, and can live better than the richest nobleman. The only
difficulty is that they will be about thirty miles from the sea; but this,
by good management, can be made of little consequence",—Pennypacker,
"Historical and Biographical Sketches", p 186 f.

and for the first ten years the use of as much more as they might want without charge, save the yearly rent of two shillings for each hundred acres. Furthermore, the settlers were not to be accounted foreigners, but allowed to possess the land as much as though they had been born there. They were to have the same privileges of religious worship as the Reformed and the Lutherans.

Such a land and such an offer appealed to the poverty-stricken, oppressed and persecuted sectarians of Germany with almost irresistible power. When to such inducements were added the letters of friends already in eastern Pennsylvania, telling of its opportunities, and the solicitations of land companies, already described, it is small wonder that in the years between 1719 and 1737 there was such a stream of emigrants from western Europe as was never before known.

Life was not all ease in this new land, but it was easier than in Germany. While some felt that the hardships incident to the emigration and settlement in Pennsylvania were too great for the benefits to be reaped, most were convinced that by diligence a good living could be made. Those that were in Pennsylvania did well for the most part. In 1733 John Nass could say of the Dunkers "they are all well off".* Thus, the economic conditions in America at this time were very attractive.

3. RELIGIOUS CONDITIONS IN PENNSYLVANIA.

The social condition that gave the political and economic forces an opportunity to make their appeals to these sturdy Germans was the religious condition of Pennsylvania. The butcheries ordered by Louis XIV in 1674 and 1688, of the inhabitants of the countries bordering on France, especially of the Palatinate, had created horror throughout Europe. The oppression of the Mennon-

*Brumbaugh, "History of the Brethren", p 120.

ites and other sectarians in Switzerland had not only resulted in driving most of these people from the persecuting countries but had induced many minds to question
the expedience of the persecutions. The story of the
sufferings of these Germans stirred the Quakers in England, who themselves had experienced the oppression of
the state. William Penn had himself known what it is to
be imprisoned for conscience' sake. His own experiences
and the reports of the persecutions on the Continent
settled within him the conviction that no country should
persecute its subjects for a religious belief, so long as
that belief did not interfere with the functions of the
state. Hence, when the King of England paid a· debt
that he owed to Penn's father with a large grant of land
in America, and an opportunity was thus given to Penn
to found a colony on principles according to his own convictions, he determined that there should be no oppression within its borders for the sake of religious belief.

As early as 1677 Penn entertained significant ideas of
religious liberty. In his letter to the Elector Palatine
in that year he set forth these conceptions in the clearest
possible manner.* This ideal of religious liberty Penn

---

*"In the first place, I do with all sincere and Christian respect acknowl-
edge and commend that indulgence thou givest to all people professing
religion, dissenting from the national communion; for it is in itself a most
natural, prudent and Christian thing.

"Natural, because it preserves nature from being made a sacrifice to the
savage fury of fallible, yet proud opinions; outlawing men of parts, arts,
industry and honesty, the grand requisites of human society, and exposing
them and their families to utter ruin for mere nonconformity, not to
religion, but to modes and fashions in religion.

"Christian, since the contrary expressly contradicteth both the precept
and example of Christ, who taught us 'to love enemies, not abuse our
friends, and triumph in the destruction of our harmless neighbor'. He
rebuked his disciples, when they wished for fire from heaven upon dissenters, it may be opposers; certainly, then he never intended that they should
kindle 'fire upon earth to devour men for conscience'. And if Christ, to

had had incorporated into the Constitutions that preceded the Frame of Government. In these he says, "Every person that doth, or shall reside therein, shall have and enjoy the free profession of his, or her faith, and exercise of worship toward God, in such way and manner as every person shall in conscience believe is most acceptable to God."*

In the laws confirmatory of his Frame of Government, passed in England, Art. 35, it is provided as follows:

"That all persons living in this province, who confess

whom all power is given, and his holy apostles refused to employ human force and artifice so much as to conserve themselves, it is an arrogancy every way indefensible in those that pretend to be their followers, that they assume an authority to supersede, control and contradict the precepts and examples of Christ and his apostles; whose kingdom, not being of the nature of this ambitious, violent world, was not erected or maintained by those weapons that are carnal, but spiritual and intellectual, adequate to the nature of the soul, and mighty through God to cast down the strongholds of sin, and every vain imagination exalted in man above the lowly, meek fear of God, that ought to have the preeminence in the hearts of the sons of men.

"Indulgence is prudent, in that it preserveth concord: no kingdom divided against itself can stand. It encourageth arts, parts and industry, to show and improve themselves, which are indeed the ornaments, strength and wealth of a country; it encourageth people to transplant into this land of liberty, where the sweat of the brow in not made the forfeit of the conscience.

"And, lastly, it rendereth the prince peculiarly safe and great. Safe, because all interests, for interest sake, are bound to love and court him: great, in that he is not governed or clogged by the power of his clergy, which in most countries is not only a coordinate power, a kind duumvirateship in government, imperium in imperio, at least an eclipse to monarchy, but a superior power, and rideth the prince to their designs, holding the helm of the government, and steering not by the laws of civil freedom, but by certain ecclesiastical maxims of their own, to the maintenance and enlargement of their worldly empire in their church; and all this villany acted under the sacred, peaceable, and alluring name of Christ, his ministry and church: though as remote from their nature, as the wolf from the sheep, and the Pope from Peter".—"*Select Works*", 2:436, 437.

*Hazard, "Annals", 1:573; Penn's "Works" 1:122 f.

and acknowledge the one Almighty and Eternal God, to be the Creator, Upholder and Ruler of the world, and that hold themselves obliged in conscience to live peaceably and justly in civil society, shall in no wise be molested or prejudiced for their religious persuasion or practice in matters of faith and worship; nor shall they be compelled at any time to frequent or maintain any religious worship. place or ministry whatsoever."*

This proclamation of liberal ideas in Penn's advertisements of his new Colony, doubtless, had much to do in attracting the persecuted sectarians of Holland, Germany and Switzerland.†

Penn found ready hearers among the Mennonites and Anabaptists of Holland and Germany, as is attested by his "Journal" of travels in those countries.‡ That his business was not limited to the preaching of Quakerism is shown by the fact that it was on these visits that he disposed of a large tract of land in Pennsylvania to some Crefelders, and that his visit led to the formation of the Frankfort Land Company. The chief appeal was, doubtless the religious liberty that could be enjoyed there.**

Futhermore, Penn went about the business of getting colonists from Holland and Germany in a systematic manner. Benjamin Furley, a Quaker from England, had migrated to Holland, and married there, was in business there, and was a man of considerable influence in that country. He had made it his concern to interest himself in the Quakers that lived in Germany and the adjacent states, to protect them in their interests, and to help

*Hazard, "Annals", 1:573.

†See list of such advertisements given by Diffenderfer and Sachse in "Penna. German Soc. Proceedings", 7:162, 175; also "Penna. Magazine of His. and Biog.", 4:331.

‡"Select Works", 2:400 f.

**Pennypacker, "Historical and Biographical Sketches", p 11.

them emigrate to the Quaker Colony. This man was Penn's agent at Rotterdam, and assisted in spreading abroad the advertisements of America.*

When the Dunkers had come to the point in their history where they were ready to leave Germany and Holland, all this was ancient history. Since 1682 there had been Mennonites in Pennsylvania from Crefield. Pastorius and others had been sending back reports to their friends in Germany.† These letters, and the persistent advertising that both Penn and the English Crown had been putting into circulation in Germany about Pennsylvania had made the conditions of religious freedom to be found there well known to the Dunkers. Hence, in an age when religious liberty was only a fitful reality, at the best, and dependent on the whim of the ruler, or the exigencies of politics, the formulation of such a proposition as Penn's with the avowed purpose of putting it into execution marked a distinct advance in democratic government, and the widespread advertisement of the plan constituted a strong inducement for the Dunkers to emigrate to this land of religious freedom.

4. INFLUENCE OF THESE CONDITIONS ON THE DEMOTIC COMPOSITION IN PENNSYLVANIA.

These conditions determined two interesting social facts in the population of Pennsylvania of that time, viz: (1) that the population was a likeminded one on most matters; (2) that it was a heterogeneous population as regards its likemindedness on minor religious matters, which at that time assumed so large a place in men's thoughts.

*See Pennypacker, "Settlement of Germantown," p 2, and "Furley" in Index.

†Ibid, p 51 f.

From the nature of the case only persons socially quite alike responded to the appeals that the new Colony made. Those that responded to these stimuli were alike in race, social station, economic condition and, to a large degree, in faith.

In race the Dunkers, Mennonites and Quakers originally belonged to the same ethnic stock,–Teutonic. Penn's mother was Dutch. The persecutions of the Mennonites and Anabaptists of Holland and Germany had driven many of them to England where they had become Quakers. That Penn in all his sympathies was a Teuton is shown by the heartiness with which he was received by the Germans and the Dutch in his journeys on the Continent in 1677.*

The political and economic conditions of all these people that came to Pennsylvania were much alike. All had been persecuted by their respective governments.† They all belonged to the middle and lower classes of society, which had neither in England nor on the Continent any political rights that the governments were bound to respect.

Between the Dunkers and Mennonites there was even a greater degree of social likeness. The only differences concerned minor points of religious doctrine. They were from the same parts of Germany. Social intercourse had been common between the two sects. A Dunker preacher preached for the Mennonites in Germany.‡ Common sufferings in various parts of Europe had driven Mennonites and Dunkers together, and had assisted the social assimilation and even amalgamation that con-

*See his Journal in "Select Work," p 400 f.

†"Chronicon Ephratense," p 3, 22, 248.

‡Ibid, p 249.

tiguity was promoting.* Economically, the Dunkers and Mennonites belonged to the same classes. For the most part they were farmers and weavers.

In religious beliefs the Dunkers, Quakers and Mennonites were very much akin. Their differences were, for the most part, on questions of emphasis. All believed it the duty of Christians to refuse to bear arms, to take oaths, and to be separate from the world in dress and customs. Dunkers and Mennonites especially held beliefs in common, the Washing of Feet as a rite of the church, the Salutation of the kiss between brethren, and the necessity of the Ban in church discipline.

Moreover, these three sects had their origin in the same general movement, the Dunkers and Quakers being, in part, historical variations of the sectarian movement of which Mennonism was an earlier manifestation.

All these circumstances, these points of similarity in customs, in racial characteristics, in class feeling, their coming from the same localities, their mutual acquaintanceship, and their common beliefs conspired to make them all recognize their mental and practical resemblance. All these tended, before proximity had made them conscious of their differences, to cause them to recognize their agreements. They felt that they were kindred peoples.†

Hence, at the distance of two continents everything made the Dunkers feel that in Pennsylvania, of all places, they would find a people most like themselves, and a place of refuge and opportunity.

Although the Dunkers did not see them before they ar-

*See Moeller, "Church History," 3:465; Goebel, "Geschichte d. Christlichen Lebens," 2:740.

†Goebel, "Geschichte d. Christlichen Lebens," 2:740 f; Cf. Mack, "A Plain View, etc.," p 72 f; Also "Chronicon Ephratense," p 249, and Pennypacker, "His. and Biog. Sketches," 26 f, 181 n.

rived in America, there were differences in the population that assembled in Pennsylvania. All the parties concerned became increasingly aware of these differences in the years that followed the arrival of the various elements of the population. On the whole the population was homogeneous. But it was just heterogeneous enough to promote discussion and a mild sort of conflict. This unlikeness was due to the minor differences in religious beliefs, in church organization, in social mind and habits of life that had developed from inherited tendencies, and in the differing environments of their former places of abode. Contiguity exaggerated these small differences. It took time and acquaintance to modify these differences and to make the people more homogeneous. It is these minor differences that come to expression in the strife between the Dunkers and Mennonites and Quakers in the years that followed the settlement of the Dunkers in Germantown. The consciousness of these social differences conditioned the lack of social cooperation that characterized this early period of the history of Pennsylvania. It was promoted by the lack of easy and cheap intercommunication between the different settlements. It produced a condition of social isolation that helps us to explain much in the early history of the Dunkers in America.

CHAPTER II.

The Early History of The Dunkers in America:
Sociological Interpretation.

Such conditions existing in America determined the settlement of the Dunkers there and influenced their early history in Pennsylvania. Conditions in Europe determined their emigration; the situation in America, having come to their knowledge, determined that Pennsylvania should be the scene of the beginning of the second period in their development.

1. Origin of the Dunker Church in America.

The Dunker church in America grew out of the Crefeld congregation in Prussia. In 1719 in response to the motives already noticed, Becker's company of about twenty persons emigrated to Philadelphia, and settled near Germantown. This was the first company of Dunkers to land on American soil. They found among the German Mennonites, already here, many persons known in the old home.

The most striking fact in the history of the Dunkers during the first two years after the arrival of this first party, is that there was no organization of the church. They were not a church, simply members of the Crefeld congregation scattered about the various settlements around Germantown as a centre. Apparently, their migration to America had been induced largely by economic motives, for the members of the company were not agreed concerning the troubles that had taken place at Crefeld, some taking the side of Hoecker and others that of Libe. Hence, they were not a social unit. There was something of the same consciousness of unlikeness among them as caused the rupture at Crefeld. Consequently, any sort of social organization was impossible.

There was a homogeneity among them, but it was not pronounced enough at first to allow them to cooperate in an organization.

Three circumstances, separation from each other, the passage of time, and contact with social elements in the population of the country unlike themselves, put an end to this condition of affairs. The first put an end to the bickering that engenders strife. As Professor Ross has noted, the social process often promotes con sciousness of unlikeness by bringing slight differences to expression by contact.‡ The isolation of the Dunkers in their new homes worked in the opposite direction. It alleviated the acute condition of social strife by doing away with the favoring circumstances. The second, the passage of time, tended to bring about the same result. This allowed these discordant elements opportunity to forget their unlikeness. They could not see each other often, and when they did, the space of time that intervened caused them to recognize and enjoy their likenesses rather than to dwell upon their points of difference. The third, contact with members of other sects, emphasized the effect of the second. By contact with the Quakers, Mennonites, the Lutherans and the Reformed in their vicinity the Dunkers became conscious of differences between themselves and these other social elements. Proximity emphasized unlikeness that distance hid from view. But by becoming aware of the fact that they were unlike the other social elements, the Dunkers became conscious of a social likeness among themselves. This contact with others, thus, developed a consciousness of kind. The result was that after about two years the consciousness of likeness was so far developed among them that it demanded expression.

‡"Foundations of Sociology," p 96.

While these stimuli of their environment were working the same results in all the Dunkers, Becker was responding to them most heartily and most rapidly. Therefore, it was Becker that first of all came to the conclusion that the disorganized condition of the Dunkers must be remedied, and undertook the first "visitation", in the interests of harmony and unity among the scattered Dunkers. This was in 1722, when with two companions, he undertook a journey, or "visitation," to the scattered members about Germantown, in order to bring about some sort of association.* These men visited the members that lived in the region known as Skippack, Falckner's Swamp, and Oley. This "visitation" had much to do with the settlement of differences, with allaying the unpleasant feelings, and in promoting that social likemindedness that resulted in the revival of religion, among these Dunkers and in the beginning of their social development in America.

The visit gave opportunity to all the scattered Dunkers to express their recognition of likeness, which had been growing for two years. Moreover, Becker had become possessed of an ideal, viz., the organization of all these likeminded people into a society in which the desire for sympathy and brotherly affection could be realized. To the other Dunkers, this ideal became a stimulus to which they responded favorably. That organization made possible further progress.

In the autumn of that year, the Dunkers, of whom Becker continued to be the leading spirit for some time, began to hold meetings in Germantown, at the homes of Becker and Gomorry. These meetings continued, until the winter prohibited the attendance of those that lived any distance from Germantown. During the winter of

*"Chronicon Ephratense," p 21 f.

1723 the meetings were held at weekly intervals. In the autumn of 1723 a rumor got abroad among the Germans on the Skippack that Christian Libe, the preacher that had occasioned the trouble at Crefeld, and who was the minister in charge there, had arrived in Philadelphia from Germany. In order to meet him a number of people from the Schuylkill country went to Philadelphia. The report turned out to be false, but on the way home these people went through Germantown, and were invited by the Germantown Dunkers to remain over Sunday with them and attend the meeting. The country people did so, and were so much impressed by what they saw and heard, that soon afterwards they made a second visit to Germantown. The Dunkers, in turn, visited them. The result was that these people applied to be received into membership at Germantown.

This application raised an interesting question. Hitherto the members at Germantown had not considered themselves a church; they were merely members of the Crefeld church. However, after due deliberation, the members at Germantown decided to grant the request of these friends from the Skippack to be taken into the church. The candidates chose Peter Becker to baptize them. This first baptism by the Dunkers in America occurred in the Wissahickon Creek near Germantown on Christmas day, 1723.*

That night was held the first Love Feast, as the service in connection with the Eucharist was called, ever held by the Dunkers in America, at the house of John Gomorry. At this Love Feast Peter Becker officiated.

Thus, naturally there grew up an embryo-organization.

*The names of these people, the first members received into the church in America, are Martin Urner and his wife (Hausschwester), Henry Landis and his wife, Frederick Lang, and Jan Mayle.—"Chronicon Ephratense," p 23.

There was no formal action taken with the definite purpose of forming an organized congregation, but when this need arose, this body of consciously likeminded people assumed the functions of an organization. They accepted certain people as members, they allowed one of their number to baptize the candidates and they held Love Feasts. Here, in contrast with the origin in Europe, we see the *spontaneous* rise of an organization to meet the request of applicants for membership. This was the beginning of Dunker organization in America. From that beginning step by step has developed the Dunker church in America, with her Annual Meeting, her district meetings, her Sunday school and missionary meetings, and her various organizations local to each congregation. The first steps towards it began with Peter Becker's efforts to visit, and to unite, on the basis of his ideal, the scattered members about Germantown. Another step in the same direction was taken when unorganized meetings were held at various places, at which the things on which they were agreed were emphasized, and their disagreements forgotten in the zeal that was begotten of their contact with unlike elements in the population of that region. But the definite step was now first taken. Now there was a Dunker church in America. Hitherto, there had been but scattered members.

These unusual events among the Dunkers excited the curiosity of the people about the neighborhood, and many of those attracted to the meetings by curiosity later became members. All the next summer meetings were kept up, until the storms and cold of winter again put a stop to them. In the spring of 1725 meetings were begun again, with the result "that the whole region round about was moved thereby".* The movement assumed the pro-

*"Chronicon Ephratense," p 23.

portions of a revival. It was a movement among the young people especially. The accessions to the church, as well as the strange manners and customs of the Dunkers, drew the attention of the people round about, so that the Dunkers' limited accommodations were overcrowded. The following summer also the meetings were continued and Love Feasts were held frequently. These frequent meetings, characterized by a ready acceptance of Becker's ideal, cultivated mental and moral likeness, which was promoted, on the other hand, by the opposition their activity excited. The brethren at Germantown sent letters to their friends in Germany, telling them of the "awakening" that had occurred, and of the good results. This correspondence, doubtless, had something to do with Mack's coming hither in 1729.

2. CONRAD BEISSEL AND HIS INFLUENCE ON THE DEVELOPMENT OF THE DUNKER CHURCH.

A. Early Period: To his Separation from the Dunkers.

In the autumn of 1720 a man sailed from Europe, whose coming hither was fraught with important consequences, in more ways than one, for the Dunker church in America. In that year Conrad Beissel, with at least four companions, arrived at Boston.

He was born after his father's death and all his early years were years of hardship. His mother died when he was eight years old, and "from that time on he led a sorry life, after the manner of the country, until he was old enough to learn a trade".* Even after he had learned the baker's trade he still was a homeless, dissipated, godless man. This hard life made a very deep impression upon his sensitive nature. While a citizen of the Palatinate, after

---

*"Chronicon Ephratense", p 3.

a dissipated life, he was "awakened", and became a Pietist.* He knew something of the Dunkers of Schwarzenau, but they were too sectarian to suit him. Besides the Dunkers, there was another party very much like them in that region. This group was what was known as the Inspirationists.† With them he worshipped for a time after his "awakening". But coming under suspicion among them he finally left their party. During this period he was under the influence of such mystical writers as Boehme.

After leading a wandering life for some time he decided on this journey to America. On his arrival at Boston, he made his way to Germantown. Here he was kindly received by some of the Dunkers. As there was no opportunity for a baker to make a living in Pennsylvania, he apprenticed himself to Peter Becker to learn the weaver's trade.

While living with Becker, he learned of the disorganized and divided condition of the Germantown Dunkers. They were not only scattered throughout the settlements, but were also divided in sentiment concerning the unfortunate division at Crefeld, Germany.‡ Their zeal for the cause had been dissipated by their quarrels. The "Chronicon Ephratense" is responsible for the statement that it was at Beissel's suggestion that the Dunkers decided to have meetings in order to bring about a settlement of the difficulties.

In 1721, after he had completed his year of apprenticeship with Becker, Beissel, in company with Stuntz, one of his fellow-travellers from Europe, went into that part

---

* "Chronicon Ephratense", p 5.

† "Chronicon Ephratense", p 1. Doubtless, these were the same as those spoken of by Goebel as "Enthusiasts".

‡ "Chronicon Ephratense," p 15.

of the wilderness known as the Conestoga country, now Lancaster county, and there they set up their solitary abode in order to realize Beissel's ideal of a hermitical life, which ideal he owed to the influence of such mystics as Boehme, Arnold, and Petersen.

While living here Beissel came into relations with several sects that had great influence on his beliefs. Thus, there was a settlement of English Sabbatarians at Nant-mill, not far away from his cabin, and he soon adopted their beliefs on the question of the Sabbath.*

Furthermore, his previous tendency to Jewish legalism was strengthened by intercourse with a community of Jews that had settled in the same valley. With Beissel's legalistic conception of the Gospel, and his austerity of character, he was prepared to respond favorably to such influences, in the absence of any sharp antagonism to those that held them. Imitation of those people confirmed his position on the Sabbath and determined his views on the eating of certain meats forbidden by the Mosaic legislation.†

Moreover, during these first two years of residence in the wilderness, Beissel in company with Isaac van Bebern had made a journey to the Labadist colony in Maryland. His views on celibacy were like theirs. He agreed with them already in his leanings towards ascetic practices, and their example found in Beissel a ready imitator, not only of their asceticism, but also of their communism. These three influences are significant in connection with Beissel's views worked out later in his Dunker congregation at Conestoga and finally and completely in his community at Ephrata.

*Sachse, "German Sectarians", 1:28, 72; 2:164; "Chronicon Ephratense", p 44; Holsinger, "History of the Tunkers", p 136.

†Sachse, "German Sectarians", 1:116.

The wilderness environment itself was a favorable environment for the development of asceticism, since it heightened rather than subdued the ascetic tendencies of Beissel. Furthermore, it was only in such surroundings that ascetic ideals could thrive. Therefore, the environment conditioned the asceticism of Beissel.

On the other hand, the composition of the population, sparse though it was, was homogeneous on broad lines, since, on the whole, the German settlers here were from the same social class in Europe and had had very similar experiences. They had come largely from the Rhine countries of Germany and Switzerland. They were men and women whom the horrors of war, with its consequences, had robbed of gladness, almost of happiness; in whom had been engendered, not only a hatred of war, but also of material prosperity and of civil power.* It should not suprise us, therefore, if Beissel found these people easily brought to much the same mind as himself on

---

*Here is a German poem by Yillis Cassel, written about 1665, which describes the condition of the Rhine country from which many of these people came:

> Denn es ist bekannt und offenbar,
> Was Jammer, Elend, und Gefahr
> Gewesen ist umher im Land
> Mit Rauben, Pluendern, Mord und Brand,
> Manch Mensch gebracht im Angst und Noth
> Geschaendeliert auch bis zum Tod.
> Zerschlagen verhauen manch schoenes Haus,
> Vielen Leuten die Kleider gezogen aus;
> Getreed und Vieh hinweggefuehrt,
> Viel Jammer und Klag hat man gehoert".—Pennypacker,

"Historical and Biographical Sketches", p 195.

And Max Goebel, writing of Wittgenstein, the region whence some of them came, says, "Das Land ist rauh, steinigt und unfruchtbar, so dass nur in den niederen Gegenden der Raggen gedeiht und selbst der Hafer und die Kartoffel an vielen Orten nur muehsam gewonnen wird; Obst waechst nur sparam in den waermeren Thaelern und in sehr geschuetzen Lagen; etc.",—"Geschichte d. Christlichen Lebens", 2:739.

religious matters, when they had been subjected to a similarly harsh environment in Europe and now to the same wilderness environment in Pennsylvania. That he did find it easy to bring a considerable number to his way of thinking is indicated by the fact that he had gathered about him an incipient congregation of people on the broad basis of combatting the irreligious tendencies of wilderness life. It was in this population that Beissel had promoted the awakening of which the Dunkers heard before they visited the district in 1724. In his hut on the banks of Mill Creek the Dunkers found him in that year living as a "solitary" with Michael Wohlfahrt, when they made their second "visitation", referred to below, to the people outside of Germantown.

So successful had the Germantown Dunkers been in creating an effective likemindedness in the people of Germantown who potentially resembled themselves, that soon most of the former had joined them. But with the consequent increase of opposition on the part of the socially unlike elements of the population, the zeal of the Dunkers grew. In the expression of their zeal they obeyed the law of least effort and sought those outside of Germantown that they believed were like themselves. Therefore, the Germantown Dunkers now resolved to make a second "visitation". Accordingly, on Oct., 23, 1724, they started. They visited Skippack, Falckner's Swamp, Oley and the new members in the Schuylkill country. From there they went on to the Conestoga country, where an "awakening" had occurred under the influence of Beissel, about the same time as that at Germantown, and where there were living some Mennonites, and Separatists.* On November 12th they held a meeting at the home of Henry Hoehn. Beissel was

*"Chronicon Ephratense", p 24.

present. Five were baptized as a result of the meeting that day, but, although he had contemplated such action, Beissel was not among them, because he felt that no one of these Dunkers was of greater ability than himself. Finally, however, he became convinced, that since Christ had allowed himself to be baptized by John the Baptist, he should humble himself and be baptized. Accordingly a short time afterwards he was baptized by Peter Becker. After the baptism a Love Feast was held at Henry Hoehn's. Three more were baptized within the week.[*] The new members in the Conestoga country were organized into a church. As the Dunkers had not yet developed a method of caring for new congregations, when Becker and his party left for Germantown, they commended the new congregation to the grace of God, and left them to their own devices. The members of the congregation proceeded by choosing Beissel as their "overseer" (Vorsteher).

It was a fateful choice, for, while the Germantown Dunkers were at Conestoga, they learned of the peculiar beliefs of Beissel mentioned above. That made them suspicious of his "orthodoxy". Their fears proved well founded, for while this congregation remained in communion with the Germantown congregation for some time, Beissel at once began to preach the importance of keeping the Jewish Sabbath, the superiority of the state of celibacy, and the shunning of certain meats for food.[†] He also showed that he was possessed of extraordinary powers, which today we should probably term hypnotic.[‡]

[*]However, the revival suddenly stopped, because of the rise of dissension over the difficulties that had risen at Crefeld.—Ibid, p 24, 26.

[†]"Chronicon Ephratense", p 27; Cf. Sachse, "German Sectarians", 1:116.

[‡]Ibid, p 35, 36. Doubtless, it was this strange power that had occasioned the rumors in the community that he was a sorcerer and a seducer of women. In a superstitious age such rumors were accepted at face value and helped to raise suspicions against him.

It is certain that during all his life he had a strange power over women, as well as over many men.* The suspicions
of the Dunkers are the first indications of a consciousness
of social unlikeness between Beissel and the Dunkers,
which consciousness of kind afterwards produced very
important results.

However, Beissel was not disturbed in his sway over
the congregation for some time. His activity, however,
was not confined to this congregation of the Dunkers.
Until he finally broke with them in 1728, Beissel held
meetings among the Dunkers in various places, as a result of which many were added to the Dunker church.
For example, in 1728 he held meetings at Falckner's
Swamp, and sixteen members were added, and a congregation organized. He also held revival meetings
among the members on the Schuylkill at which many
were added to the church. Moreover, his activity was
not confined to the Dunkers, but included all the Germans in the vicinity.

For three years the relations between Beissel and the
Germantown Dunkers were seemingly friendly. But the
suspicions that had been aroused in the minds of the latter on the occasion of their visit to the Conestoga congregation in 1724, when Beissel was baptized, were never al-
layed, and the lack of frequent communication prevented
social assimilation. The absence of mutual confidence
finally led to an open rupture. It came about in the following manner: Jacob Stuntz had married a kinswoman.
Beissel condemned the marriage as improper and had
Stuntz and his wife put under the ban of the Conestoga
congregation. In 1727 some of the Dunkers of Germantown made another "visitation" to this congregation. On
the way Henry Traut and Stephen Koch stopped to visit

*See, Sachse, "German Sectarians", 2:89, 91, 118.

Stuntz and his wife. After hearing from them the story of the trouble, they proceeded to remove the ban from them without waiting for action by the congregation. This was irregular, and, at a meeting held at Henry Hoehn's, Beissel had them disciplined for removing the ban on their own responsibility. Naturally the Germantown Dunkers sided with Traut and Koch. This occasioned hard feelings between Beissel and the visitors.*

The next year after the organization, during Beissel's meetings, of the congregation at Falckner's Swamp, the Germantown Dunkers endeavored to prejudice the new congregation against Beissel. This resulted in further bitter feeling and an incipient division between the "Beisselainers" and the Dunkers of Germantown.

Moreover, a division occurred in the congregation at Conestoga, fostered, as Beissel's party thought, by the Dunkers of Germantown. Michael Wohlfahrt went to Germantown and rebuked the congregation, and Peter Becker in particular. Thus, was a consciousness of difference developed.

Further, Beissel laid emphasis on celibacy, which the European experiences of the Germantown Dunkers, as a church, made them unwilling to endorse. All these events made each side recognize the fact that it was unlike the other. With these various elements still unassimilated by time and custom, and with the recognition of the unlikeness by each side to the controversy, the proper conditions were present for a rupture. It came about, formally, in December, 1728, when Beissel had himself and all his followers baptised over again and thus "gave the Germantown Baptists back their baptism", as he said. This he did, because the latter were saying that

*"Chronicon Ephratense", p 36, 38.

he had received his baptism from them, and therefore all he was he owed to them.*

In the following year, Alexander Mack and his large company of followers arrived at Germantown from Westervain, West Friesland. In this company were 126 persons,—59 families,—some of whom settled at Germantown.†

What was the immediate cause of the emigration of this company of Dunkers under the leadership of Mack from Friesland to Pennsylvania it is impossible to say with certainty. In general, the causes were much the same as moved the other sectarians to leave Europe at that time for the Colony of the Quakers.‡

The Dunkers in Friesland had already broken loose from their native country, and, after the years of wandering they had experienced, the ties that bound them to Europe were not strong. The congregations in Europe were scattered. Political and religious liberty was not assured them any length of time. The economic opportunities of the New World, according to all reports that reached them, were much superior to theirs in Friesland. In fact, there was every reason for their leaving Europe and going to Pennsylvania.

The addition of these new members from the other side of the sea made the Germantown church a large one, and gave a great impetus to the work there. It not only added numbers, but it created a congregation in which

*"Chronicon Ephratense", p. 48.

†It is not certain, however, that all these were Dunkers. It is probable that most of them were, however, as Dr. Brumbaugh has compiled a list of 116 members that came with Mack to America.—"Pennsylvania Archives", Second Series, 17:18; "Chronicon Ephratense", p 16; Brumbaugh, "History of the Brethren", p 54 f.

‡Nass's letter translated in Brumbaugh's "History of the Brethren", p 108 f; "Chronicon Ephratense", p 24.

the recently arrived Dunkers were in such a majority that it was virtually a new congregation. The new members before arriving at Germantown had become assimilated into a social unit that gave great stability to the Germantown congregation. Furthermore, this immigration brought to the Germantown church Alexander Mack, a man of the greatest influence among both the "Beisselainers" and the Dunkers. The weight of his influence enabled him to use his wise counsel in the settling of any differences, and in directing the work of the church, while he lived.

Naturally, when he arrived, the first thing he heard of was the recent defection of the "Beisselainers". But he heard the story only from the Germantown side. In 1730 he, with some of the Germantown members, made a journey to Conestoga for the pupose of healing the breach between the two factions. But Biessel was in no mood for compromise, and the negotiations came to naught. Some time afterwards Beissel wanted to drop matters and have a reconciliation, but the Dunkers would not consent without a previous investigation. To this Beissel would not consent. Thus, the division became permanent.*

As we look at the matter from this distance of time, it is apparent that there was error on both sides. What seem to us trivialities, were exaggerated into causes of offence by the imperfectly united parties to the controversy.

The underlying cause of the division was the consciousness of unlikeness that existed in two parties. Beissel had more of the mystical element in him than the Germantown Baptists could look upon with favor. He was certainly a man of extraordinary gifts, but a man also of great self-esteem, and he was under the influence of the

*"Chronicon Ephratense", p 31,32.

mystics whom he had met in Germany, rather than of the men that controlled the Dunkers. As the authors of the "Chronicon Ephratense" remark, "those who know how the affair stood between the two congregations, know also that a close union between them was impossible; for they were born of diverse causes". That is the real explanation of the beginning of the trouble and of the final rupture. *"They were born of diverse causes"*,—not only in the sense intended by the writers, but of *diverse sociological causes*. The leaders and the congregation had developed under different environments. Beissel had been subjected to a more mystical environment in Europe. He was under the influence especially of the mystical writings of Boehme and later of Gottfried Arnold, while Mack had been influenced by the latter's historical writings only.

The rough life that Beissel had always led made him susceptible to this mystical influence. Furthermore, he had not been a Dunker in Europe, he had joined the Inspirationists. He knew of the Dunkers, but they had had no influence upon him there. He was not acquainted with their ideals and their mode of worship, except in a general way. Experience of their mode of life, of their way of transacting business, and of their ecclesiasticism Beissel lacked. He had not experienced the evil effects of communism, which experience had made the Dunkers react against that feature of church life after seven years of trial in Germany. The year that Beissel had spent with Becker in Germantown was before the Dunkers commenced religious services. Therefore, Beissel was utterly without experience in Dunker church life, when at the close of his year with Becker he went out into the Conestoga wilderness.

On the other hand, in that region his contact with the

English Sabbatarians, the Jews and the Labadists and his imitation of them exaggerated his already existing social unlikeness to the Dunkers.

All such influences were lacking to the Germantown Dunkers. By Mack and his followers the mystical was looked upon with suspicion. Also, their experiences with communism and celibacy in Germany had not been such as to cause them to look upon the experiment in America with any degree of favor. Furthermore, the fact that they were organized prevented the adoption of many doctrines that some members may have favored. Environment, experience, numbers and organization all united in determining that the Dunkers at Germantown should not agree with Beissel's views.*

This division brought new influences to bear upon both the "Beisselainers" and the Dunkers. The hard feelings between them were deepened, when some from each side went over to the other side. The influence that the less mystical Dunkers had hitherto exercised over the adherents of Beissel was cut off, and Beissel's influence, tending to make the Dunkers more mystical, ceased to act upon them. Beissel came no more into their meetings, and leading Dunkers, like Mack and Becker, visited Beissel's followers less frequently than before, although members of the two congregations still mingled occasionally.†

What the result would have been, had the two groups continued freely to react upon each other we can only conjecture. It is probable that the Dunkers would have become more mystical, and the "Beisselainers" might

---

*I have dwelt upon this first and most fateful division in America, so far as the early days are concerned, because it has never been explained, and because of its influence negatively on the later history of the Dunkers.

†"Chronicon Ephratense", p 95.

have given up some of their mystical tendencies. Social homogeneity might have been achieved in due time. However, the differing situations of the two congregations, the one in settled Germantown, and the other in wild Conestoga, tended toward differentiation, although it might not have ended in division, if they could have been kept united until after civilization had transformed the wilderness.

As a result of the separation, the Dunkers reacted against the mystical, and laid more stress on the Scriptures while the "Beisselainers", although revering the Scriptures, continued to rest more heavily on the immediate guidance of the Spirit, especially as revealed in Beissel.* Henceforth, the two parties, representing the two tendencies that had been combined in the Dunker church at the time of its origin at Schwarzenau, were clearly differentiated. Each went its own way. The one became the developing Dunker church; the other a small community that was doomed to die with the passing away of the wilderness environment that had cradled it.

The sociological significance of the history up to this point is that it illustrates the theory of social causation that we have traced in the earlier history in Europe. The character of the Conestoga wilderness conditioned the kind of people that went there. It attracted men like Beissel, who wished to get away from other men, live in solitude with God, and mortify the body. Therefore, it was a home for mystics and fanatics. It attracted people that wanted an isolated region in which they might work out their peculiar ideas, like the Sabbatarians. Men that had failed elsewhere, as well as the more adventurous sought it out. And, finally, it attracted some men

*"Chronicon Ephratense", *passim.*

that were too poor to settle in places where the land was higher in price.

Socially the inhabitants were an unformed mass. There was no political association to draw them together. The environment had determined that many of the inhabitants of the region should be susceptible to such ideals as Beissel's. As soon as enough people were assembled in the Conestoga country the instinctive response of each to the difficulties of his environment suggested association with the others. The common dangers, economic necessity, and the inherited social instincts all prompted it. This led to instinctive associations, such as were realized in neighborly visits. But instinctive association soon led to purposive association of an unorganized character, such as co-operation in building a hut or clearing and sowing a field. By such means social intercourse was developed, and the way for discussion was opened. People with a past history such as most of these people possessed naturally soon came to the discussion of religion, because of the sadly neglected state of religion in the wilderness. This talk suggested the holding of wholly unorganized religious meetings to remedy the sad state of affairs. In these meetings, of course, such a man as Beissel, a man of superior natural gifts and wider experience, took the lead by common consent. Thus, partly instinctively, partly purposely, grew up the first unorganized religious associations, in response to an ideal that had resulted from social tradition and discussion.

The past experiences of the people who agreed that a revival of religion was needed had been only sufficiently alike to permit agreement on the general need. On the more specific questions of the things to be taught and the kind of organization needed there was variety of opinion. Beissel responded most quickly and energetically to the stimuli of his wilderness environment and to the secondary stimuli presented in the ideals of the Sabbatarians, Jews, and his fellows in Conestoga as well as to the suggestions of men whose teachings he had read and heard. Reacting on this situation in Conestoga Beissel conceived of a sort of organization to conserve the religious interests of the community. Thus, sprang up the organization of the congregation at Conestoga.

At first it could not yet be called Dunker, because Beissel was not yet a Dunker. Probably the best description would be to say that it was a congregation of mystical Pietists.

On the first visit of Becker and the Germantown Dunkers, another and more definite ideal was presented that resulted in some, at least, of this congregation becoming Dunkers. Whether the whole congregation responded to this ideal or not we are unable to say. It was this Dunker congregation, modified according to the peculiar ideals of Beissel, that he left, when he went to Ephrata.

Its importance for us is that it shows us the process by which a social organization comes into being. The material environment determined the population of the country where it originated. The population of the Conestoga region conditioned the sort of organization demanded, at first but loosely united on some general principles only. Later a presentation of a new ideal by the Dunkers and the lack of competing ideals determined the more compact organization on the narrower lines of an organized Dunker church.

b. *Later Period*: *Beissel's Separate Community.*

For about seven years Beissel had charge of the Conestogo congregation.* In 1728 Saturday was adopted by

*"Chronicon Ephratense", p 63.

this congregation as the Sabbath. Hitherto Sunday had been devoted to the services, and Saturday was kept in quiet.* In the same year the formal rupture was made by Beissel, who "gave back their baptism" to the Dunkers, as he said, by having all his adherents baptized over again. About the same time a revival occurred.†

In 1732, perhaps in March, Beissel suddenly left the congregation, after appointing some elders to take charge and giving them a New Testament with which to govern the congregation, and went eight miles to the northwest, to the place now called Ephrata, which was then a wilderness, and took up his abode in a small hut that had been built by Emanuel Echerle. In September of that year, however, Beissel called together the heads of the congregation of Conestoga, to consider the affairs of the church at that place. Reports had come to him that things there were going badly. Beissel now practically assumed control of the congregation again. Soon afterwards several of the unmarried men and women of the congregation at Conestoga followed Beissel to Ephrata. There gradually grew up about him at that place a settlement that has become famous in American religious history.

About 1732 by means of an "awakening", aroused by the efforts of Beissel, in the Tulpehocken church, a union congregation composed of Lutherans and Reformed, but under the care of a Reformed pastor, Beissel obtained an opportunity to present his views to that people. He won over to his side the pastor, Peter Miller, one of the most learned men in America at that time, and Conrad Weiser, a man of wide influence, an elder in this congregation and an authority on Indian affairs, who on this ac-

*Ibid p. 44.

†Letter in "Geistliche Fama", 1731, Drittes Stuech, p 21. (In Penna. His. Soc. Library.)

count stood in high esteem with the government.* Through their influence and that gained by his success in promoting the revival among them Beissel was enabled to win over to his peculiar views two other elders, the schoolmaster of the congregation, and "about ten families" of the membership of the Tulpehocken church.† Not later than May, 1735, these were all baptized and joined the church over which he had presided before he left for Ephrata, and over which he even yet exercised practical supervision ‡

The reasons for the change are to be found in the conditions of the country, and the personality of Beissel. In an age of loose morals in the church, as well as outside of it, it was natural that men of the deep seriousness of these Germans should revolt against sexual sin. But their reaction against this sin led them to attack matrimony by a very common logical error. This austerity, developed in Germany in reaction against the loose morals of the time, was strengthened by what they saw of domestic conditions in America. It was often the custom in the wilderness of Pennsylvania for a man to have two wives. Contemporary records present us a picture of morals that is anything but elevated.** It was in reaction against this state of things that Beissel adopt-

*See, "Colonial Records", Index, "Conrad Weiser".

†Boehm's letter in "Minutes and Letters of the Coetus in Pennsylvania", p 8.

‡Boehm says April, Ibid, p 2, 3, 8; cf. "Chronicon Ephratense", p 73. These people did not move to Ephrata, however, until some time later. This change on the part of Miller and a portion of his flock was not a sudden one, but the outcome of about five years of friendly intercourse between him and Beissel. Already in 1732 Miller had gone to the house of one of Beissel's followers and joined with them in the rite of Feet Washing.

**Cf. Mittelberger's "Journey to Penna., in the year 1750" trans. by Theo. Eben: Philadelphia, 1898.

ed the suggestions of the German mystics and ascetics. In so doing he was simply responding to the stimuli of his environment. That the experience of Beissel was shared by many others is shown by the numbers that he was able to get to respond to his ideals. This wilderness of Conestoga provided all the favorable conditions that enabled Beissel's followers to realize the ideals unhindered.

Moreover, it was a time of great religious uncertainty in Pennsylvania. To those that were used to the settled religious usages of Europe, the conditions in America seemed to verge on heathenism.* All sorts of sects were tolerated, and sprang up everywhere. As most of the people had come to Pennsylvania to escape from religious intolerance, it was but natural that in the atmosphere of toleration there they should sometimes go too far in their new found freedom.

People were unsettled in religious matters. Coming from a land of despotism and from thickly settled communities into a land where each one was free to be religious or not as he pleased, and into a country sparsely settled, the absence of the usual moral and religious restraints loosened rigid habits, and made some men careless of religious customs that hitherto had been matters of course.

Coming from a land where school and church privileges were provided for them without thought or care, on their part, to a land where all had to be provided at their own cost, they neglected these matters, when they had all they could do to make a living. There were few preachers and schoolmasters. They had no one to guide them in religious and moral affairs.

*See the dialogues between the traveler and the farmer in Sauer's "Almanacs", Penna. Historical Society Library, Philadelphia.

Furthermore, religious deadness, coupled with memories of a different state in other days, made these people susceptible to such an "awakening" as Beissel knew how to promote. The circumstances of their wilderness life made them defer to the power of the few strong characters with whom they came in contact. Already affected with Pietism many were open to Beissel's message. These facts, with the dominating personality of Beissel, and their frontier life account for the notable accession of members, which so strengthened Beissel's cause at this time of need.

In 1734 members of the congregation at Falckner's Swamp, which Beissel had so large a part in organizing, began to move to Ephrata, that they might be near Beissel, "so that in a few years the country for from three to four miles around was occupied by this kind of people".*

In 1735 for the unmarried female followers of Beissel the communistic mode of life began to supplant the hermitical mode. Hitherto those that had followed Beissel to Ephrata had lived each in his own separate hut. Now the first building for common use was begun. Some of the married followers of Beissel contributed what property they possessed to the fund for the erection of other buildings.† The male "solitary" brethren established the communistic life in 1738.

Soon after this Beissel began to urge upon the married people the necessity of practising continence. A great many of them separated from their husbands and wives, the men living in one apartment, the women in another. The families that refused to break up had their own household economy in the settlement. They did not mingle

*"Chronicon Ephratense," p 66.

†Ibid, p 79, 81.

with the unmarried, for the latter were considered holier than the married. In this household of the married eating at common tables was introduced.* The "solitary" life with which Beissel started out thus became a communistic life. This change was the result of the reaction of these people upon the conditions of life where they lived. The institutions that grew up were the product of response to certain external stimuli, which made up, in part, the environment. In Beissel's case, as at Schwarzenau, Germany, the communistic life was the result of reaction on harsh social conditions. More than any of the Dunkers he had been a wanderer. The hard European experience of Bessiel as a child and young man, and of his neighbors of Ephrata, was repeated by him and most of his congregation in America. They lived on the frontier, with the terrors of savages and wild beasts about them, and an untamed wilderness between them and civilization. The virgin forest had to be cleared away before they could begin to raise their crops. The cultivation of the land was difficult because of the lack of implements and domestic animals. Even after he and some of his friends had moved to Ephrata they drew the ploughs themselves, probably because of the lack of horses or oxen†.

Furthermore, it is a common observation that pioneer communities are hospitable. They have not that grasping disposition characteristic of older societies. They are more open to the needs of men, wealth is not hoarded so closely, and private property has not yet become so strictly private. Frontier life seems to make men more

*Ibid, p 83, 90.

†A later age thought it was from humane motives, but the explanation of the text is much more likely, as they later used oxen and horses in the fields. They hitched themselves to the plow for the same reason that they went on foot in their journeys, because they had no other way.

considerate of the needs of their fellowmen in certain
matters. The dangers of the wilderness and the un-
certainties of existence tend to promote the communistic
form of life, for they make cooperation necessary. The
communistic settlement at Ephrata was cooperation on a
large scale.

This mode of life, however, was the result of response
not only to the stimuli of the material environment, but
also of the opposition that they experienced from those
about them who had misunderstood their aims, or were
displeased with their practices. The eccentricities of
Beissel's people attracted the attention of members of
other faiths. Their practice of celibacy, their monkish
dress, their sectarian tendencies raised suspicions against
them. Their neighbors thought them Jesuits, and free
lovers, and invented all sorts of strange stories about
them. This made sharper the social differentiation of
the "Beisselainers" from the other inhabitants of the
region, and tended to increase their zeal for their ideals
and to favor the communistic life. The whole situation
was just such as to favor the imitation of ascetic and communistic ideals, if not, indeed, to suggest them. The isolation of the region and the community from outside influences prevented interferences with the realization of
Beissel's ideals.

That the communistic features of Beissel's settlement
at Ephrata were products of the response of the Community to the stimuli of the environment is indicated also
by the fact that the communism died out when the wilderness gave place to civilization.

An organization never develops very far before its leaders formulate and seek to enforce a policy of uniformity.
This is done for the purpose of assisting the process of
social assimilation. It may take the form of a policy of

uniform language, religion, culture or even a uniformity of dress. In this case a uniform language, religion and dress was adopted.* In 1735, or 1736, the unmarried men adopted a uniform garb. In this they were soon followed by the unmarried women, and finally by the families, or "domestic household". In this way the leaders of the Community sought to realize the ideal of unity.

In 1736 the Dunkers of Germantown made a "visitation" to the Community at Ephrata. Notwithstanding the fact that Beissel once before, since he had formally separated his congregation from them, had refused to have anything to do with them, the Dunkers desired to bring about a reconciliation. Beissel, however, refused to allow his people to accept the overtures of the Dunkers.† This was the last attempt to unite the two parties.

In 1737 the "Solitary brethren" at Ephrata came into conflict with the civil authorities over poll taxes. They refused to pay them, on the ground that, like the ancient Egyptian ascetics, they ministered to the poor of the neighborhood, and that, therefore, like their Egyptian prototypes, they should be excused. After some trouble about it, in which the brethren were locked up in the Lancaster jail for ten days, the Commissioners and Assessors of Taxes, consented to remit the poll tax on condition that the "solitary brethren" should pay taxes on the land they held.‡ How illuminating is this incident! Living in a wilderness far from civil authorities, living their own life, what was government to them? All they had on which to base an opinion of civil authorities was the memory of a government that oppressed them. Notice, moreover, their ground for refusing to pay the poll

*"Chronicon Ephratense", p 182.

†"Chronicon Epratense", p 95, 101.

‡"Chronicon Ephratense", p 87.

tax,—they were doing the same work as their Egyptian prototypes. They felt themselves akin to the early Christian ascetics, therefore they lived thus and refused to pay the tax. Here clearly appears the reason for their imitation of early Christian asceticism and monasticism, viz., consciousness of kind growing out of a like response to a similar environment.

About 1736 or 1737 a revival began in Germantown. This revival, like most of the "awakenings" among the Dunkers at this time, was characterized by enthusiastic and ecstatic phenomena. But Becker and Nass opposed the revival on account of the observed consequences of such revivals in Germany.* In consequence of the opposition, a number of those that had been "awakened" at this time, and some of those who had promoted the revival, left Germantown, and joined the party of Beissel at Ephrata.†

Naturally, the desertion of these persons, among whom were two children of Mack, the founder of the Dunker sect, and several members of the original band of Schwarzenau, caused hard feelings. The defection is interesting, because it shows that, although the Germantown church was growing away from the ideals of life with which it had started out in Germany, and was becoming more orderly in its methods, there were some among its members that had not shared in the evolution. Their attitude shows a return to the ideals of an earlier time, and reveals the fact that social assimilation was

---

*Cf. Davenport, "Primitive Traits in Religious Revivals", *passim*.

†The names of the married people in this party of seceders were, "Henry Kalkglaesser, Valentine Mack, John Hildebrand, Lewis Hoecker, Pettikofer, the widow of Gorgas, and their children". "To the solitary belonged Henry Hoecker, Alexander Mack Jr., John Reissmann, Christian Eckstein, Elizabeth Eckstein, Martha Kinsing, and Miriam Gorgas".—"Chronicon Ephratense", p 101, 102.

not yet complete. Although some of these converts to
the ideals of Beissel returned to the Dunkers later on,
yet the falling away caused a widening of the already
existing breach between the Dunkers and the followers
of Beissel. That feeling had run high between Mack and
Beissel as early as 1731 is shown by the notice of events
in the "Geistliche Fama", which says that Mack had
written a book against Beissel's view on the Sabbath.*
While for some time a feeling of kinship continued to
exist between individuals in each party towards individuals in the other, the separation now became more pronounced, and finally complete, even in feeling. From
this time on each party went its own way. That some
of these converts later returned to the Dunkers shows
that two ideals were in conflict at this time among these
Germans, and that a process of selection was determining
the issue of that conflict. History and the wilderness
were with Beissel; experience and advancing civilization
were on the side of the Dunkers. The future belonged to
the party at Germantown. That the latter stood against
the reactionary tendency shows that a new day in Dunker history was dawning.

The defection of Beissel and his party from the Dunker
church resulted, thus, in the separation of the two different conceptions of life that had been held simultaneously,
more or less loosely, by the Dunkers from the beginning
of their history in 1708. The ascetic conception, that of
Beissel, had originated in a time of harsh experiences. It
was the practical response of an oppressed people to the
stimuli of an unfavorable environment. The other conception, that of the main Dunker party at Germantown,
was the fruit of a more settled history. Hitherto, both
had existed side by side in the Dunker church, now the

*Drittes Stuech, 1731, p 51.

one and now the other predominating, according to the circumstances of the time. Here they became clearly differentiated. That Beissel still held to the ascetic, ecstatic and communistic ideal meant that the Dunkers ceased to hold it. This came about for two reasons: (1) because a consciousness of unlikeness determined that the Dunkers should refuse to hold what Beissel and his followers believed; (2) because, consciousness of kind selected the members from each party according to the ideal held by that party. That was the significance of Beissel and his community for the history of the Dunker church. His separation from them meant the definite and final repudiation of his ideals. That repudiation determined that the Dunker church should not be a celibate and communistic community, subject to the domination of the Spirit in one man, but a church organized on democratic principles, living its life in the world, and governed by the Spirit of God working on the hearts of all its members. Therefore, the influence of Beissel upon the development of the Dunker church was very significant.

The followers of Beissel built up the Community at Ephrata step by step until it attained considerable importance in the life of the frontier. Beginning with a bake-house and public granary, they soon added to the plant a saw and grist mill, a woolen mill and paper mill. There was also a tannery and a pottery furnace. As early as 1745 a printing press and a book bindery were established.[*] All this industrial advance was made while the Community was under the control of the Echerlin brothers and for the purpose of supporting the Brotherhood of unmarried brethren, who had hitherto been supported by the offerings of the Community. After the dethrone-

[*]"Chronicon Ephratense", p 140 f ; Brumbaugh, "History of the Brethren", p, 456.

ment of the Echerlins and the return of Beissel to the
ascendancy, these signs of progress, which were looked
upon as "worldly" by the most of the members, were
allowed to fall into decay or were burnt down. The members, moreover, had groaned under the Echerlins' severely industrial and commercial policy.* The money
that was accumulated under the wise management of
these able brothers and which had been loaned out by
Israel Echerlin, the Prior of the Brotherhood in Zion, as
the unmarried male members were called, was now soon
dissipated by Beissel in gifts to beggars and in paying the
debts of false members.† The fine orchards that the
Echerlins had planted were rooted up.‡ The industry
that had been built up went to nothing. In spite of the
fact that there were accessions from different quarters
at various periods, the beginning of the decline of the
Community dates from this period. The Echerlins had
seen which way the logic of events was leading. They
endeavored to meet the new situation and adapt the Community to the changed environment. But they were in a
minority. The circumstances demanded that the Community enlarge its scope to meet the needs of a developing country. When it decided to remain stationary, the
Community sealed its own doom.

Confirmatory of this is the number of unmarried brethren and sisters in the Community at different times.
Thus, when in 1738 the community life of the "solitary"
brethren was established, 17 "solitary brethren" moved
from their huts into Zion and became the Zionitic Brotherhood, a kind of monk's Order. In 1740 there were 36
single men in this Brotherhood and 35 single women in

*"Chronicon Ephratense", p 139, 170 f., 209 f.

†"Ibid, p 199-205, 137.

‡Ibid, p 193.

the corresponding Sisterhood. About 1745 there were approximately 70 persons in both orders, besides the "household" economy of the married members and their children, of which at one time there were nearly 300 members in the vicinity. In 1746 there were 34 single brethren, while the next year there were 80 members that belonged to the orders. In 1764 there were 21 males and 25 females. In 1769 there were but 14 males in the Brotherhood. This is the last we hear of the exact number of the unmarried men and women. When this celibate feature of the Society disappeared we do not know. Sometime before 1865 the Brother-house was occupied by sisters, hence before that time the Brotherhood must have ceased to exist.

Not only the celibate orders died out, but the membership in general decreased gradually after the middle of the eighteenth century. In 1769, according to Dr. Fahnestock, a member of the community, there were but forty families, with 135 members all told including both the celibate men and women and the households. Of these 14 were male celibates.

In 1830 at a meeting of the Society, a motion was passed that the Society should allow members to vote by proxy on account of the inconvenience of attending the meetings. This shows that the members were becoming widely scattered. In 1827, the first date from which minutes have been preserved, there were but 20 men and 15 women that attended the business meeting of the Society. In 1839 only 20 members voted; in 1843, the number had dwindled to 13. After this date the voting membership rose to 14 in 1847, 22 in 1855 and 29 in 1875. In the summer of 1904, when I visited the Community, the celibate mode of life had entirely disappeared and the membership about Ephrata was limited to twelve or fifteen members. The only trace of the communistic feature remaining was the ownership of the property by the Society, which is controlled by a board of trutees.* There the old buildings stand, which expressed the hopes of earnest men and women to establish a place where the warring, selfish, and sinful tendencies of the wicked world should be shut out. It was a dream, the splendor of which, in the eyes of these people, is attested by the serious way in which they went about to realize it. But it was a dream that the composition of the population round about made unrealizable. They had to learn by hard experience, that no man and no community can live unto itself. The great unfriendly world pressed in upon Ephrata ·dimming its glorious vision, and finally overcame it.

Yet, in spite of the strange events that marked its history and this reversion to a mode of life whose day was past, the Ephrata Community was a light in a great wilderness, not only in spiritual affairs, but also in matters industrial, educational and charitable at a time of great need in the history of Pennsylvania. Her buildings were gladly devoted to serve as hospitals for the wounded soldiers of the Revolutionary Army after the battle of Brandywine. She had one of the first schools in all that country. Her printing establishment was one of the earliest and best that printed in the German language in America.

The further history of this interesting experiment it is not our purpose to follow. The important steps in its history have been noticed. Its origin as a voluntary association to remedy religious indifference in the wilder-

---

*Holsinger, "History of the Tunkers," p 139; "Chronicon Ephratense," p 106, 192, 193; Minutes in possession of the Trustees of the Society at Ephrata; Rupp's "History of Lancaster County," p 217.

ness and its development into a Dunker cogregation has been traced. Its development as a congregation in the adoption of the Sabbath, and of a Jewish legalism, and its emphasis on celibacy were noticed. We then saw the steps by which its history was separated from the Dunkers and the further development from a church into a community. The social development of this Society was then traced from a simple unorganized collection of like-minded people into a completely organized body with a well developed constitution and a unified policy. The critical period in its development was then noticed, when it turned back from the path of industrial development marked out by the Echerlins, and its subsequent gradual decay.

It remains only to explain its decadence. After Ephrata was transformed from a wilderness by the advancing tide of civilization and became a comparatively well settled place, and after the physical environment made possible a different intellectual and religious life, the Community began to lose its influence and power. Some have thought that it went down because Beissel's successor, Peter Miller, was not the equal of the former as a manager of the Community. On the contrary, in every respect, except in the eccentric personality of Beissel, Miller was vastly his superior. He was one of the best educated men in the Colonies. He had the solid characteristics of the best Germans. His temper was much more even and his eccentricities much less pronounced. He was not so erratic and overbearing. And, finally, he had none of Beissel's petty vices. The reason for the decadence of Ephrata lay not so much in the difference in the two men that stood at its head as in the changed circumstances of its social surroundings. The crisis was reached, when in 1745 the Community turned its back upon its opportunity to welcome the new era that had dawned socially in the Conestoga wilderness. Then was its chance to become an industrial centre and contribute to the development of the country in which it was located. It chose to revert, however, to the religious self-centralization characteristic of its earlier history, and in so doing failed to adapt itself to the changing conditions of its environment. In time a process of natural selection destroyed it.

Thus, Ephrata arose in response to a need felt by certain elements in the population on the frontier of Pennsylvania. But, when the wilderness receded before population and civilized conditions, when peace succeded war and oppression, and when, instead of a grudging reward for patient toil, the land yielded bountifully, and there was an unlimited demand from outside the community for what it produced, the stimuli that had created the community ceased to act. Its ideals died with the environment that gave them birth.

In Germantown, with its more heterogeneous composition, the ascetic and mystical Dunker heritage, brought from Germany, was sloughed off sooner than it was in the wilderness at Ephrata. A gradually changing environment, differing stimuli, increasing differences in the composition of the groups, and therefore gradually differing ideals,—these facts make up the explanation of the two diverging developments of the same historic movement.

CHAPTER III.

EXPANSION OF THE DUNKERS IN AMERICA.

As we saw in the last chapter, the Dunkers had no sooner arrived in America than they scattered to various parts adjoining Germantown. However, it was only when land became dearer in Eastern Pennsylvania that they sold their farms there and sought new and cheaper ones in the south and west. This movement of the Dunkers from the places where they first settled to newer portions of the country is described by the title at the head of this chapter.

This expansion must now be traced in some detail. Up to 1770 the following churches had been organized besides, doubtless, some scattered members elsewhere.

The first Dunker church to be organized in America, the one at Germantown, in 1770 had 50 members in 40 families.

In the previous chapter the origin of the Coventry church, the second in America, was noticed. It was organized in 1724, with nine members.* In 1770 it had 70 members.†

A few days later the Conestoga church was organized. This was the one over which Beissel was elected teacher, an event that occasioned the trouble between Conestoga and the Germantown Dunkers. Eleven of the Conestoga members went with Beissel. Twenty seven, however, remained in allegiance to the Dunkers of Germantown. There has always since been a church at Conestoga, or as it is sometimes called, Cocalico. After Beissel's defection, Peter Becker ministered to this church until

*Brumbaugh, "History of the Brethren", p 274; Cf. "Chronicon Ephratense", p 22.

†Ibid, p 296.

1734, when Michael Frantz was placed over it. At this time there was a reorganization of the congregation. In 1734, or 1735, this congregation had 20 members; in 1747, or 1748, it had 200 members*; and before 1790 it had received a total of 463 members.† In 1770 there were 53 families connected with this church, comprising 86 persons in full communion.

It appears from the "Chronicon" that there were small numbers of Dunkers at Skippack, Falckner's Swamp and Oley as early as 1722.‡ These places were on the route often taken at that time from Germantown to the Conestoga country.

In 1770 there were 20 members at Oley. Its formal organization seems to have occurred late, but doubtless there were members there from the first, as this was one of the places at which Becker and his party stopped in their first "visitation".**

According to Edwards, the Great Swamp congregation was organized in 1733.

In the same year the congregation at Amwell, New Jersey, was organized, although probably some of the members who formed the nucleus of these two congregations had settled in these places previously.

The White Oak congregation, which was near the Conestoga church, was organized in 1736, although already in 1729 there had come into that region several persons from Germany, some of whom probably later became members.†† This and the Conestoga congrega-

*Cf. Brumbaugh, p 299.

†Chronicon Ephratense, p 118; Record said to have been written by Peter Becker, quoted by Holsinger, "History of the Tunkers", p 429.

‡"Chronicon Eph." p 24.

**Brumbaugh, "History of the Brethren," p 297.

††Ibid, p 318.

tions were under one elder.   In 1770 it had 65 members, according to Morgan Edwards.*

In 1738 the Little Conewago congregation, in York county, Hanover township, was organized.   In 1770 it had 40 families with 52 members.

In 1741 the Conewago congregation, 14 miles from York, was established.   In 1770 there were 77 members here.

In 1748 the Northkill congregation was organized, made up of members in Tulpehocken and Bern townships, Berks county.   In 1770 there were 11 members.

In 1756 the Great Swatara congregation was organized, but its first member had been baptized there in 1752.   In 1770 it had 39 members.

The Bermudian congregation, in York county, was organized in 1758.   In 1770 it had 40 families with 58 members.

In 1758 the Codorus church, in York county, was organized.   In 1770 it had 35 members.

As early as 1760, there were a few members in the Carolinas, when Daniel Letterman and Casper Rowland moved thither from Germantown, Pennsylvania.

In 1762 the Stony Creek church, in Somerset county, came into existence.   It was the first congregation west of the Alleghanies.   In 1770 it had 17 members.

In 1770 the Little Swatara congregation was formally organized, although already in 1745 several people had settled there who afterwards became the first Dunkers in the place.   In 1770 it had 45 members.

Thus, in 1770 there were 15 congregations of Dunkers in Pennsylvania with a total membership of 623 and Beissel's congregation at Ephrata with 135 members. Also there was one church in New Jersey, at Amwell, which in 1770 had 28 families with 46 members.   Morgan

*"Materials towards a History of the Baptists in America", Vol. on Penna.

Edwards states in 1790 that there were 7 churches in Maryland, and 10 in the more southern states.*

A close study of these early congregations reveals the interesting fact that the congregations nearest to Germantown began to suffer from emigration very early in their history. Thus, the Germantown church in 1770, with a history of forty seven years, had only fifty members, and the Coventry church had only forty members left after forty six years, while the Conestoga congregation, which up to 1770 had received three hundred and ninety five persons into membership, had but eighty six members remaning at that date. These congregations are simply illustrations of what had happened to all the Dunker churches in the older parts of Pennsylvania in 1770. Where they had gone is partially shown by the statement of Christopher Sauer, when, in his letter to Governor Denny in 1755, he said that there were then, "eight or nine counties of German people in Virginia, where many out of Pennsylvania are removed to".†

This first period of expansion was checked by the outbreak of the Revolutionary War. But at the close of this war, when the Indians of the Northwest Territory had been subdued, and the last signs of British rule along the Lakes had disappeared, the cheap lands of Ohio attracted the Dunkers thither from Pennsylvania, by way of Pittsburg, and from Virginia and Maryland, while some Dunkers crossed the mountains from Carolina into

---

*"Materials towards a History of the Baptists in Jersey"; Cf. Brumbaugh, p 335. In this account of the state of the church in America in these early days I am indebted to Morgan Edwards' works, written from 1770 to 1790, and especially to Dr. Brumbaugh's excellent work on the subject in his "History of the Brethren", Chapter 9; Cf. Holsinger "History of the Tunkers", Chapter 7.

†See translation of Sauer's letter in Brumbaugh, "History of the Brethren", p 380, or Holsinger, "History of the Tunkers", p 787.

Tennessee and Kentucky and thence reached Indiana and Illinois. From Ohio the churches spread westward to Indiana and Illinois, and thither westward to Iowa, Kansas, Nebraska, the Dakotas, and the Pacific slope.

From the Carolinas Dunkers crossed into Kentucky and preached there at a very early day.* Before 1800 Dunker settlements were made in Simpson, Muhlenberg and Shelby counties, Kentucky, by settlers from Ohio, Virginia and Pennsylvania.†

As early as 1799 settlers from Virginia crossed into what is now Greenbrier and Washington counties, Tennessee. But the number was small until 1833, when a number of families came from Virginia. From that time on a stream of Dunker emigrants kept pouring westward from Virginia and the Carolinas into Tennessee and Kentucky.

The first Dunkers came to Missouri in 1795 from North Carolina and Pennsylvania. In 1824 there were fifty communicants in Cape Girardeau county and they were closely connected with a Dunker settlement forty miles away in Union county, Illinois. The Dunker churches of southwestern Missouri have been organized since 1870.

In 1808 Jacob Wolfe and George Wolfe Jr. moved from Kentucky to Union county, Ill. The next year George Wolfe Sr., then of Logan county, Kentucky, whither he had moved in 1800, from Fayette county, Pennsylvania, preached in southwestern Missouri and Illinois. But the first Dunker church was not organized in Illinois until 1812.‡ The Dunker settlements in northern Illinois were

---

*The Dunker, Joseph Rodgers, is reported to have been the first white man that preached the Gospel in Kentucky.

†Holsinger, "History of the Tunkers", p 762.

‡Ibid, p 402 f.

made by people from Indiana and Ohio, for the most part, and were later.

About 1800 Dunkers began moving into Ohio. John Caylor and family at that time moved into the Miami valley from Virginia. About the same time Dunkers came into the Mahoning valley also, the first named valley being in the south western and the other in the north-eastern part of the state. In 1829 some Dunker families moved from Montgomery County, Ohio, into what is now Elkhart County, Indiana. At the same date there were Dunkers in Union County, Indiana.*

James R. Gish and other Dunkers emigrated from Virginia to what is now Roanoke, Illinois in the fall of 1849. But an earlier settlement of Dunkers had come into Illinois from Tennesee and Kentucky. There were Dunkers in Illinois as early as 1824. About 1850 there were Dunkers in Du Page, Lee, Ogle, Stephenson, Adams, and Union counties, at least.

According to the statement of David Peebler, of Oregon, the first Dunker church in Iowa was organized in 1840, or 1841, in Jefferson County. The date when the first Dunkers arrived in that state is unknown, and whence they came. In 1852 a family of Dunkers moved to the region near where Maquoketa now stands, in Jackson County. In 1854 Dunkers settled in Linn County, Iowa, and in 1856 the church south of Waterloo, Iowa, in Black Hawk County, was organized. In both the latter cases the settlers were from Pennsylvania, the former from Blair, the latter from Somerset County.

Thus, in Ohio, Indiana, Illinois, Missouri and Iowa the two streams of Dunker migration, the one by the way of Maryland, Virginia, the Carolinas, Tennessee and Ken-

*Holsinger, "History of the Tunkers, etc.," p 334, 401.

tucky, the other through western Pennsylvania, Ohio and Indiana, once more met.

In 1867 there were Dunker people at Salem, Albany and Lebanon, Oregon. The first members probably settled in Oregon in 1852, going from Illinois across the plains and mountains in wagons, and settled eight miles above Oregon City.*

As early as 1856 we find Dunker members in California, whither they had moved from Illinois.†

This account of the spread of the Dunker people is by no means complete. Nevertheless, it is all that published material, so far as I am aware, will enable one to say about the early development, and it enables us to get a fairly complete conception of the distribution, if not of the numbers, of the Dunker migrations up to the time of the Civil War.

This movement took place in response to the economic motive. The other causes that moved them to migrate to America were no longer operative. Desire to better their condition financially, was the only cause that led them to forsake communities already fairly well settled, to seek the frontier, to turn their backs upon church and educational privileges for themselves and their children, to hide themselves in the forests and mountains of Pennsylvania, Virginia, Maryland, the Carolinas, Tennessee, Kentucky, and the prairies of the Ohio and Mississippi valleys.

The direction of this expansion, however, was determined by other factors in addition to the economic. The physical character of the country was one thing that determined where the Dunkers went. If the reader will take the trouble to follow geographically

*Holsinger, "History of the Tunkers", p 185, 812.

†Ibid, p. 752.

the multiplication of congregations from the parent congregation at Germantown, he will discover that growth was determined by physical conditions, both in its direction and in its extent. In these early days travellers and emigrants followed the line of least resistance, the natural watercourses. Such was the route that Becker and his party took in their first "visitation" in 1722. Subsequent Dunker migration followed the Schuylkill River into Montgomery county and into Berks county, to the head waters of the Conestoga River, which flows southwest into the Susquehanna. This river was then followed up into the Cumberland valley, thence the route led down into York county, and through Maryland, to the Virginias and the Carolinas. Another path of migration, however, instead of turning into the Cumberland Valley, continued up the Susquehanna, to the Juniata, up to its head waters, and thence by a short portage to the head waters of a branch of the Ohio.* But the southern course was the more feasible and most of the Dunker churches before 1800 are found from Germantown to Virginia, with a few in the Carolinas, Kentucky, Tennessee and Missouri. These regions were on the line of least resistance for emigrants in search of agricultural lands, and these early Dunkers were, for the most part, farmers.†
Furthermore, the adaptability of a region for agriculture

*Semple, "American History and its Geographical Conditions," p 60; see Map, p 54.

†Penna. Ger. Soc. Proceedings, 6: 321, 360. The first Annual Meeting of the Dunker church to be held outside of Pennsylvania, Maryland and Virginia was in 1822, when it was held in Ohio. It was first held in Indiana in 1848. That was the fourth time it had been held outside of the states first named and the other three exceptions were occasions when it was held in Ohio. This shows that the great part of the Dunker membership was located in Pennsylvania, Maryland and Virginia for some time after the Revolutionary War. See "Classified Minutes," p. 398; Brumbaugh, "History of the Brethren," p. 491.

had a decisive effect on the direction of their migration.

Thus, these Dunkers spread abroad and settled in the Schuylkill, Susquehanna, Cumberland and Shenandoah valleys, because they were well adapted to the agricultural methods of that day. Moreover, they looked for fertile valleys. These Germans had been the best farmers of Europe and when they sought new homes the superior fertility of the western and southern valleys had an effect on their decision. Again, the proximity of the Cumberland and Shenandoah valleys to the seaboard led the Dunkers to occupy them rather than the equally fertile valleys of western Pennsylvania.

Another factor in the determination of the direction the expansion took was the social. Between two places equally good from the economic standpoint, people choose that one where there is already a population like themselves socially. This consideration determined that, once a bold spirit had chosen a region from other considerations, the rest of his comrades in faith chose that region rather than some other, because of their consciousness of kind.

It was consciousness of likeness, begetting an affection for their fellow countrymen and co-religionists and a desire to supply to them the blessings of the church, that led to "visitation" of members in outlying districts and the organization of scattered members into churches. From that day in 1772, when Peter Becker organized the first "visitation" to the scattered brethren living in eastern Pennsylvania, until in recent years a different policy was begun with the establishment of the Indian and Persian Missions, respectively by the Conservative and the Progressive branches of the general body, missionary work has always been conducted on the "visitation" plan. Growth has been by means of emigration and colonizition. A few members, for the sake of better economic opportunities, have broken away from a congregation, and migrated to another place, where land has been more abundant and cheaper. There they have formed the nucleus of a new congregation. Hence, Dunker communities have risen along the natural routes of migration. Philadelphia was the port to which they came from Germany. Germantown was the first stop. From there colonization moved along the paths of communication to the west and south.

However, the method is striking only by reason of the fact that it is a method that in an earlier day was characteristic of many sects, to a less extent. The circumstance that it marked the method of Dunker expansion in a superlative degree and has continued down into the present is due to the fact that their customs, inherited from their German progenitors, social habits, language and peculiar beliefs exaggerated their consciousness of kind and postponed their assimilation to the social type of the place where they lived.

That fact is the chief explanation of why this great expansion of the Dunker population did not turn out disastrously for the church. In most cases such a vast dissipation of the members of a church into the wilds of a new country would have meant the loss of all these members.

Another thing that saved the Dunker church from that result was that she got her preachers from the ranks and they still remained farmers or artizans after they became preachers. In most cases each little group of Dunkers that settled in a country had at least one preacher among them. The multiplicity of ministers in the older congregations, creating petty jealousies, naturally resulted in the less successful minister emigrating to some place where his labors would suffer less from the

competition of abler men and be more keenly appreciated.
It often happened, indeed, that the colonist was the
preacher, since, until recently, all Dunker preachers have
been farmers, like the other members.

Several circumstances, promoting the isolation of the
Dunkers, conditioned the continuance of this method.

Until recently, the German language, which promoted
the consciousness of likeness and differences, has been
the language of the Dunker home. In some homes it
still holds its own, but English in the newspaper and in
the schools is too strong a competitor to be resisted. Not
many years ago, I heard a German sermon in a Dunker
church, but it is a rare thing now.

Like their language, their peculiar faith, has set the
Dunkers apart from their fellowmen. Settled in colonies
or communities, their faith and their language have led
them to convert or to "buy out" the people around them,
if possible.

One further influence, which has been effective in
strengthening the Dunker consciousness of kind, has
been the printing press. From the very beginning of
their history they have believed in the power of the
press. Even in Germany they printed Mack's defence
of their peculiar doctrines.* Christopher Sauer set up
a press in Germantown, which, although it was not
avowedly in the interests of the Dunkers alone, yet
was for the Germans, and tended to unite them in
matters of common concern. It also was used by Sauer
to promote the tenets of the Dunker faith. Beissel at
Ephrata set up a press for the propagation of his views.
There was a period in the early part of the last century,
indeed, when literary activity among the Dunkers seemed
to wane, but today they have a literature of their own,

*Holsinger, "History of the Tunkers", p. 45.

which they use effectively to spread their views and to develop a substantial likemindedness. All these facts, promoting a consciousness of kind, have given to Dunker expansion a method that has attracted the attention lately of many observers, but which is remarkable only because of its survival into the present, its employment to the exclusion of other methods, and its dependence on an isolating environment for its continuance.

It was inevitable that this passion for new lands and the consequent spread of the Dunkers over so broad a territory should have some evil results. There is no doubt that this scattering of the membership, weakened the eastern congregations at a critical time, tore members away from the influence of the church and isolated them in back-woods communities and retarded the socialization of the Dunkers for a long time. It also hindered their Americanization in language, education, manners, dress, beliefs and organization.

1. It set back the Americanization of these Germans in the matter of language, for just at the time when civilization was catching up with their homes in the East, bringing English schools and neighbors, the temptation to sell at high prices and go West where they could buy cheaper land proved overwhelming and again isolated them in the wilderness and prairie. The result was that they were now separated from even the few educational influences of their home in the East, the German school, contact with their better educated ministers, and Christopher Sauer's newspapers and almanacs.

The strong consciousness of kind and their isolation prevented the displacement of their native tongue by the English for many years. Thus, as recently as 1889 the Eastern District of Pennsylvania was granted their petition by Annual Meeting to have the minutes of the latter printed in common German.* On the other hand, both these influences made them cling to their language, but the isolation was just sufficient to shut them off from influences that would have kept their German pure, yet not sufficient to prevent borrowing from the English about them.

2. Likewise, the expansion of the Dunkers impeded the education of the children of such families as moved to the frontier. The Dunkers of Germantown and Ephrata were interested in schools for the education of the young. Christopher Sauer helped to build the first school at Germantown and was one of its trustees for many years.† His German almanacs and newspapers were eagerly sought by Germans from Pennsylvania to Georgia. But, it is significant that the only Dunker books printed until after the middle of the nineteenth century were published east of the Alleghanies and with but few exceptions in or near the centers of population, Philadelphia and Baltimore.‡

There is a great hiatus in the intellectual development of the Dunkers from 1784 to 1850. The reason for it lies in the expansion of the Dunkers westward into the great American wilderness and prairie. It was a period in which all the energies of these people were exhausted in making homes for themselves and in following the lure of economic opportunity. They had no time or energy to give to the higher things of life. The untamed wilderness demanded the individual attention, not only of the adults, but also of the children and therefore education fell into disrepute.

*See "Classified Minutes" of 1886-1892, p 13, Art. 14.

†Holsinger, "History of the Tunkers, etc"., p 267; "Chronicon Ephratense", p 216.

‡See Hildeburn, "First Issues of the Pennsylvania Press."

Another thing to be remembered is that they were widely scattered. Education is largely a social product, the incentive to which is the result of social contact. But contact with an educated, likeminded people was lacking. Therefore, imitation of the better educated people about them could not occur.

Moreover, on the frontier there were few educational facilities. Social organizations existed only in spontaneous forms and among these simple forms were few schools. The thoughts of the people were devoted to matters that had more direct connection with personal safety and means of subsistence. German schools for educating their children the Dunkers did not possess, and had they possessed them, they would have seen no need of them in their wilderness surroundings. The English schools were few and poor. Therefore the children grew up with only enough education in either language to enable them to conduct necessary conversation, and to read the Bible in one language, generally the German. This was the period of transition from German to English as the language of the Dunkers. The process of transition operated to produce ignorance and neglect of education. The first Dunker book in English I know of was published in 1833 and the first Dunker newspaper in English in 1851. These were the first harbingers of the coming change in the language and culture of the Dunkers. It was in 1850 that the first Dunker book on theology in English, Nead's "Theology," was published. All these circumstances exaggerated the Pietistic tendencies latent in Dunker circles against education.

3. Isolated in German settlements on the frontiers these sturdy Germans clung to their ancestral customs and manners. Their ancestors had been common peasant people with the manners and customs of that class.

Their situation in scattered communities in the West perpetuated these peculiarities and helped to retard the change to American habits. The fact that these frontier congregations were too remote from the main body of the church to share in the development for long periods explains many of the divergencies of practice in the church. For example, the two modes of Feet Washing, discussion over which subject threatened to disrupt the church at one time and gave occasion for grave discussion and legislation by many Annual Meetings, originated in the early period of Dunker expansion, before the constitution and practices of the church had been developed very far. Moreover, this period of Dunker history gave rise to the variety of Dunkers known as the Far Western Brethren of Kentucky and Illinois. They were simply a local variety of Dunkers that had not shared in the general development of the main body but had undergone a development of their own.* To this period also can be traced the different customs observed in the eating of the Lord's Supper. Some held that the only kind of meat used in the supper should be lamb's flesh.

4. Taught to believe that plainness of dress was a sign of godliness, they had every reason to continue so to believe in their backwoods' life in the settlements scattered far from the centers of culture and refinement. Hence, their enviroment again retarded the civilizing influences of dress.

5. In like manner, their isolation from other elements of the social population was complete enough to preserve intact their beliefs and practices. In doctrine this was a period of stagnation. The traditions of the fathers was the test of . orthodoxy. The passion for

*For details in regard to this movement see Holsinger, "History of the Tunkers", p 762.

social unity also operated in favor of this tendency.

6. The spread of the Dunkers had a similar effect on their social organization. Development in this line took place in the East first and then gradually enveloped the churches on the outskirts. Had the Dunkers confined themselves to Pennsylvania there is no doubt that the completion of their social constitution would have come much sooner than it did, and doubtless would have been somwhat different. The frontier congregations carried with them the ideal of the simple organization with which they were familiar.

However, the development of the constitution of the church was going on rapidly in the regions where the congregations were close enough together for frequent contact with one another. As soon as two or more congregations began to have relations with each other the evolution of the constitution of the Dunker church began.

At first it was spontaneous and sporadic, e. g., the visit of one congregation by members from another. That was its beginning. Hence, the beginning of the development goes back to the first "visitation" made by Peter Becker and his fellows from Germantown to their unorganized companions in faith at Coventry and Conestoga in 1723.

The organization of a definite inter-congregational assembly, however, did not occur until 1742. Then, it arose specifically as an instrument of protection of the Dunker congregations from what their leaders felt was a snare set for them in the Synods of Count Zinzendorf, who had come to Pennsylvania to quiet the strife between the various sects thereby organizing them all into a "church of God in the Spirit", wherein each should be allowed perfect liberty to believe and practice what he wished, but in which each sect should respect the beliefs of the oth-

ers, and cease their quarreling over theological and ecclesiastical differences. After the third Synod the Dunker
representative from Coventry, George Adam Martin,
went back to his congregation and reported to his elder,
Martin Urner, that he thought the Count's Synods were
for the purpose of enticing people back to infant baptism
and the "Babylon" of the established churches. Together they decided to "get ahead of the danger, as some
Baptists (Dunkers) had already been smitten with this
vain doctrine, and to hold a yearly conference, or as we
called it, a Great Assembly (Grosse Versammelung), and
at once fixed the time and place.''* This was the beginning of the first inter-congregational "Big Meeting" of
the Dunkers, out of which has grown the Annual Meeting, the organization that governs the Dunker church,
in all matters of doctrine and practice.† Adoption of it
is an instance of the process of conflict by imitation.
Its ultimate cause was consciousness of kind.

Before 1778, or, possibly 1791, these "Big Meetings",
as they were always called before 1832, did not meet reg-
ularly year by year.‡ At first these meetings were simply for conference and devotion. There was always held
in connection with them a Love Feast, and the settlement
of difficulties was only a minor matter. They were not
meetings in which legislation binding upon all the congregations was passed. That conception of them came
only with the lapse of time. At first, they were simply
advisory. Many times they met without having to settle
any difficulties at all. In such cases they were devoted

*See "Chronicon Ephratense", p 245.

†For a very good chapter on the origin of Annual Meeting see Brumbaugh, "History of the Brethren", p 471 f.

‡However, George Adam Martin seems to imply that in 1757 already they
were held annually. See "Chronicon Ephratense", p 245. Cf. Holsinger,
"History of the Tunkers, etc.", p 809; Brumbaugh, "History of the Brethren", p 490.

entirely to preaching and devotions. Thus, before 1830 the minutes of these mettings are incomplete. None are known to exist from the period before 1778. In 1859 the first committee, the names of whose members have been preserved was sent by Annual Meeting to a local church to settle difficulties. The first Standing Committee of Annual Meeting whose names have come down to us was that of 1785.* It was not until 1882 that the constitution was so far developed that the decisions of Annual Meetings were declared to be mandatory, i. e. binding on the local churches. Until 1868 the constitution of the Standing Committee, the very centre of the whole organization, remained practically on the same basis that it had when the Dunkers borrowed it from the Zinzendorf Synods. Its members were elected, not as since then, by the districts, but by the local congregation where the Meeting was held. Even to this day the method of getting queries to the Annual Meeting is based upon the method that was invented and used in the Zinzendorf Synods, viz., through the Standing Committee, not through individuals.†

Why did the Dunker organization develop so slowly? The reason, I think, will be found in the scattering of the Dunker forces in their expansion over the new lands of the United States. The development of the social constitution of any people is dependent upon close and frequent contact. The depletion of the congregations in the more thickly settled communities through emigration of the members to new communities hindered the development in the former, while the development in the latter had to wait on growth of population, and of means of communication and association.

*"Classified Minutes", p 382, 388.

†See Brumbaugh, "History of the Brethren", p 479.

In all these ways the effect of the spread of the Dunkers was to retard their socialization.   While in the end it resulted well for the church, for the time being it impeded her progress and brought about the conditions that made inevitable all her trouble.* From one point of view, this period might fitly be called the period of stagnation of the Dunker church.   From another point of view, this was the time of her preparation to take her place among the useful Christian denominations of America.   Expansion impeded the evolution of the Dunker church, but it made possible greater things when the process of socialization once began.

Thus, in culture, doctrine, customs and organization the expansion of the Dunkers impeded progress.

*See Brumbaugh, "History of the Brethren," p 528 f.

CHAPTER IV.

The Unification of the Dunkers after their Expansion in America.

The term "unification", as used in this chapter, signifies the process by which the Dunkers developed into a voluntary, cultural society, with a common culture, common beliefs, common purposes, and a unified organization to which the members gave loyal adherence. This is a part of the process of socialization, of which the other part is liberalization, to be treated in the next chapter.

In explaining the origin of the sect in Europe in Part I, the early steps in that process have already been noticed. Some of these steps were repeated here in America, but many of them were not. The aim of this chapter is to show how the Dunker church developed from a people who were held together rather loosely by a feeling of likeness to each other and by an antipathy to those different from themselves, and who existed in scattered congregations here and there throughout the various sections of America, into a closely united organization with a well developed social constitution, a well defined body of beliefs, and customs, and a membership very much alike in feelings, thoughts and purposes. In order to do so, it will be well to summarize briefly the stage of social development reached by the Dunkers before their expansion in America.

The spread of the Dunkers over what is now the United States resulted in arresting the process of socialization that had begun before their expansion had really commenced.

While the spread of the Dunkers had been going on from their first arrival in America, it did not assume such proportions as seriously to interfere with their natural social development until the great movement to the West, subsequent to the Revolutionary War, began. Their expansion previous to that time had been largely to the South, into the Valley of Virginia and adjacent valleys so that communication between the congregations was possible. When, however, the great outpouring of people to the cheap and fertile lands west of the Alleghanies commenced, intercommunication was not possible on the same scale as formerly, until, after the lapse of a considerable time, railroads and post lines were opened up from the East into these regions. Accordingly the social development in the East was retarded and in the West it was stopped entirely for a time.

The Dunker population in America in 1790 was not more than 1463 persons.* These were scattered in thirty-three congregations, from Germantown, Pennsylvania to South Carolina.

After the first few years, the growth of the Dunker population was by natural increase. At first, and to a small degree always, the increase of membership came from the German settlers near them, who had no church of their own confession in the immediate neighborhood.† Therefore, the growth of the membership was slow, in spite of the fact that Dunker families were large. Another thing that worked in the same direction was that during this period of expansion, in fact, since the Dunkers had broken with the followers of Beissel, they had had a prejudice against revivals. And, again, their absorption in the task of making homes on the frontiers tended to draw their interest away from an increase of membership. The result was that, when the great expansion began at the close of the Revolution, the Dunker

---

*See Chapters III and VI.

†Holsinger, "History of the Tunkers, etc.," p 475.

membership was just sufficient in its ratio to the other elements of the population to start their social development.

The Dunkers had gone through the steps in the development of the social mind that are known as like response to the same stimulus, attainment of mental and practical resemblance, consciousness of kind and concerted purposes of a sort, before they had left Europe. Their social experiences in America, up to the period of expansion, had brought them only a little beyond the point of development reached in Europe. Communication between the various congregations of Dunkers close together, association in occasional Love Feasts, and co-operation in the "Big Meetings", at which people were often in attendance from far distant congregations for the Love Feast, or, for the settlement of some trouble, or the decision of some question that had risen in that local church, helped to develop a reciprocal recognition of likeness that was beyond the point hitherto reached in the development of the social mind.

As for the social organization, at this time it had also progressed a step beyond the development reached by the organization in Europe. This advance is evidenced by the adoption of a conference to meet annually, in imitation of Zinzendorf's Synods, in order to defend the Dunkers against the danger of being seduced from their peculiar doctrines and strict sectarianism. The conference they adopted was a purposive association that had for its aim the preservation of Dunker doctrines and ideals. It resulted in a further development of Dunker organization. Furthermore, it fitted admirably into the custom, that had risen of visiting neighboring congregations and holding Love Feasts, which custom had originated spontaneously in the earliest days of their history in

America in the desire of Becker and his fellows to gather together the scattered Dunkers into an organization.* However, at the time of which we now speak, this development of the organization had not proceeded far beyond that half-purposive, half-spontaneous stage, just noticed, which existed as early as 1742. Thus, the character of the decision of the first Annual Meeting, whose decisions have reached us, was that of advice in regard to a local case. The meeting was still called a "council" and the decision a "counsel."† The ideal of unity however, was just beginning to take shape, which ideal is always prerequisite to the development of organization.‡

As soon as the churches in the older East had recovered from the effects of the dispersion, and other social elements began to crowd in upon the Dunkers, social development began again. As always, it began with a change in the conditions of the population.

1. The conditions of social development lie in *the population*. Its density, and its homogeneity or heterogeneity determine whether the society shall be a developing or a stagnant one. The families were large and were brought up in the church. Consequently, the Dunker population tended to be homogeneous. One thing however, worked against this tendency. The congregations were scattered over so wide an expanse of country and the means of communication were so meagre, that variations in social type arose. Thus, in

*See Chapter II, Part II.

†"Classified Minutes", p 206, 216, 247, 282, 347, 350.

‡"Classified Minutes", p 269, 278, 353, etc., "It has been concluded in *union*". "We have considered and weighed the matter *in union*." "For the Spirit of God leads into all truth and *union*".

the years following their spread there arose local varieties of Dunkers, such as "the South Carolina brethren," "the Thurmanites," "the John A. Bowman Church" and "the Far Western Brethren."* The homogeneous membership resulting from growth of membership by natural increase accounts for the predominant passion for unity characteristic of this period. On the other hand, the variations gave that measure of heterogeneity that demanded measures of coercion towards the individual. These facts provided conditions of progress.

Furthermore, the growth of population about them had an influence upon their social progress. It provided the unlike social element that developed consciousness of kind and gave rise to conflict of opinion, that drove the Dunkers to the defence of their doctrines and customs and to the perfecting of their local congregational organizations.†

2. The development of the *social mind* of the Dunkers, in the period following their expansion, was chiefly in the matter of concerted volition.

For some time after the scattering of the membership, the consciousness of kind already developed in Europe and America, while perhaps just as strong in the local congregation, had no chance to grow in the larger circle of brethren scattered over the larger territory. Soon, however, letters began to be sent back and forth and visits were made between churches situated along natural routes of travel. On occasion, when it became known that a "big meeting" was to be held at a certain church for the settlement of a difficulty or for the purpose of discussing a question of interest, or even simply to hold a love feast, those that were near enough attended.

*See "Classified Minutes," p 135, 341, 345, 356.

†There are no statistics of Dunker population from this period.

Here through social intercourse and, by means of conflict, toleration and imitation, the consciousness of kind was strengthened and concerted action was taken in various matters. Thus, in the first Annual Meeting whose minutes we have preserved, "After much reflection, in the fear of the Lord it has been *concluded in union* that the brethren who have taken the attest should recall it before a justice, and give up their certificate, and recall, and apologize in their churches and truly repent for their error, etc."* Many more examples might be given of the same tendency to develop concerted action on the part of those congregations so situated that they could get together. Then, as connection with the congregations scattered throughout the West was established, this same process was repeated. However, the greater social development of the region east of the Alleghanies, as well as the greater number of Dunker congregations there, determined that the social development of the Dunkers should proceed most rapidly there. Consequently, it was in that section that concerted volition developed first among the Dunker congregations.

The mode of likemindedness found among the Dunkers of this period of socialization was formal, or dogmatic. In this likemindedness there were two factors,--belief and deductive reasoning.† The Dunkers had received as traditions certain dogmatic doctrines and certain church rites, or customs. They defended them by a process of deductive reasoning, as did all the other churches of the time. What these were has been noticed in Chapter II, Part I.

Now, the effect of the spread of the Dunkers upon these beliefs was, (1) that their rationalization was postponed,

*"Classified Minutes", p 269.

†See Giddings' "Inductive Sociology," p 145 f.

and (2) that opportunity was given for differences of belief and custom to arise. The result was that the likemindedness could not develop into the next higher stage,
the deliberative. Therefore, when about 1850 conditions
became such that the long separated congregations could
communicate and associate together, they became conscious of the fact that, while they all agreed as to their
mode of concerted volition, they found in different congregations, in widely separated parts of the country different beliefs in existence. They had no sooner discovered this fact, however, than there arose in their minds
the ideal of uniformity of belief and practice. It was
such an ideal that led to the great development in organization that took place in this period, which organization
was the machinery by which uniformity was to be realized. Moreover, this passion for unity accounts for the
developments that occurred in the doctrines of the
Church. For example, the article of belief as to dress was
indefinite. All that was demanded was that it should be
plain. In defining, at a later time, what plainness meant,
however, uniform garbs were finally adopted for the
women and officers of the church, and a uniform way of
wearing the beard and combing the hair was prescribed
forthe male members. Their morality was made uniform
negatively, i. e. all members were to refrain from certain
actions, such as making or selling intoxicants or tobacco,
keeping slaves, wearing gold, attending certain amusements, etc., through the whole catalogue of negative, Pur-
itanical virtues. To break the uniform rule of morality
came to be punishable by exclusion from the Church.
The Minutes of Annual Meeting at first were considered
merely as advice or counsel, but after the social development had gone far enough a policy of coercion was adopted and the decisions became mandatory, and acceptance

of them a test of fellowship.* The later position was impossible in the early days, because the means of communicating traditions and traditional usages were imperfect, but with the growth of railroads, travel was facilitated and it became possible to have every congregation of the church represented at the Annual Meeting.

Before the rise of the church papers the Dunkers felt the necessity of devising the plan whereby the decisions of Annual Meeting might be disseminated. They therefore proposed to create a committee of "several brethren that are experienced and sound in the faith, and send them, two and two, with the decisions of the Annual Meeting, and let them visit all the congregations in the United States, and establish them all in the same order according to example (Acts 15)".† Although this plan was not adopted it reveals the consciousness that some plan must be found to make the church one in doctrine and practice. About 1851 the "Gospel Visitor", the first Dunker newspaper since the days of Christopher Sauer, was originated.‡ This and other papers, which soon arose in the church, provided a means for the easy communication of the ideals held by the majority of the members, and developed the formal likemindedness that had characterized the Dunkers throughout their history. The appeal to tradition was made in the earliest minutes of Annual Meeting that have reached us, and had been made even before this, according to George Adam Martin.** It grew

*Cf. the decisions of 1805, 1848, 1865, 1882 in "Classified Minutes," p 28, 31

†Art. 8, 1849, "Classified Minutes", p 28.

‡Holsinger, "History of the Tunkers, etc.," p 351 f; "Classified Minutes", p 323 f.

**See "Chronicon Ephratense", p 245, "Always appealing to their predecessors, saying the old Brethren in Germany did so and we must not depart from their ways".

ever more insistent as the years went on and as the means of communication improved. Thus, the two instruments whereby the dogmatic likemindedness was cultivated were the Annual Meeting and, of less importance in this period, the church papers.

3. The most important development in the Dunker church in this period was that of the *social organization.* While the growth of population and the development of the social mind were necessary conditions of the development of the organization, it is undoubtedly true that the latter had a most important reciprocal effect upon both the former. So complex are the processes by which a society grows that now one is cause and the other effect, and now the relation of the two are reversed.

Before 1742 there was no organized or regular relations between the various Dunker congregations. There were only occasional visits back and forth. From that time there was an annual gathering called by the Dunkers at that time and for many years to come "a great assembly" (eine grosse Versammelung.)* Up to this time the local congregation was the church. Development had not gone far enough to demand a further organization. But with the growth of numbers and population it was inevitable that the Dunkers must determine the organ for the realization of the higher unity that was beginning to assume prominence in the social mind.

There were three spheres in which the development of their social organization proceeded, the local congregation, District Meeting and the Annual Meeting.

The local congregations' development consisted chiefly in the changes that occurred in the ministry. On the basis of the self-governing local church that existed among them in Germany, with preachers chosen from

*"Chronicon Ephratense", p 245.

their own ranks, there gradually evolved the three degrees of the regular ministry and the diaconate.

In the Minutes of 1856, Art. 20, is found the first reference to what was called the first degree in the ministry. The article runs thus, "Is it the rule and order among the Brethren to forward a brother to baptize at the same time he is put in the ministry? Ans.—No." This shows that it had become the custom to make a distinction between the duties of ministers who had been for a longer or shorter time respectively in office.* In 1864 the question first came clearly before Annual Meeting, "What authority have we in the New Testament for three orders or grades in the ministry"? This question was deferred for answer to the next Meeting with the recommendation that "the Brethren examine the Scriptures upon the subject." It was answered thus, "We have plain Scripture to teach a grade of offices in the church. (See Eph. iv, 11): 'He gave some, apostles; some, prophets; some, evangelists; and some, pastors and teachers' ". Thus, the development in the office of the ministry that had been going on since a very early period of their history in America, came to official completion by this decision of the Annual Meeting. The duties of the first degree ministry were set forth in the form of installation prescribed by the Annual Meeting of 1874, Art. 8. According to this his duties are not onerous. †

*This practice probably grew out of the earlier practice in Pennsylvania of putting a man into the ministry on trial.—Brumbaugh, "History of the Brethren", p 391.

†He is authorized "to exhort and to preach as an assistant to the elder and older ministers, as they may give him liberty to do so. It is his duty, however, faithfully to attend the meetings of the Church, and, when liberty is given, to exhort or preach, and do it humbly, and willingly, and faithfully, as the Lord will afford him grace to do." In case none of the older ministers should come to the appointment, it is his duty to proceed with the service according to the usual order of the Brethren to the best of his ability, but

In the same year a form of installation was formulated for the second degree ministry also. The duties of this office are more important.*

The form for the ordination of an elder, as the third and highest degree in the ministry was called, was not adopted by the Annual Meeting until 1877. His duties are carefully defined and are very important.†

he cannot make any appointments for service on his own account. He can, however, preach funerals without the consent of the older ministers. He must dress according to the custom of the church and adhere to the general order of the brotherhood in all matters of nonconformity to the world. He cannot baptize or officiate at the Lord's Supper except with the consent of the older ministers.—"Classified Minutes", p 103, 104.

*He was authorized by the Church "to appoint meetings for preaching, according to the general order of the Brethren, to administer the ordinance of Baptism, and, in the absence of an elder, to take the counsel of the church on the admission of a candidate for baptism, to serve the communion in the absence of any elder, or, at his or their request, if present; to solemnize the right of marriage according to the laws of the State and the usages of the Church. In brief, to perform all the duties of an ordained elder, except that you have no authority to install officers in the Church, neither by giving a charge, as I am now doing, nor by laying on hands in ordaining a brother into the full degree of the ministry. You have also no authority to preside in the council-meetings of the church in which official members of the church are to be dealt with. You have no authority to go into the acknowledged territory of any organized church to make appointments for preaching unless called by the elder or council of said church." Furthermore, he must submit himself to his elder and be amenable to the church in all things.—"Classified Minutes", p 107.

†"In ordaining you an elder, the church gives you all the right and authority belonging to the ministry, such as presiding in council-meetings in which official members are tried, at home or abroad; if you are called to do so, in District or Annual Meetings; to give the charge to deacons, or ministers, and install them into their respective offices." It was his duty, furthermore, to be subject to the elders, or bishops, older than himself, to manifest no arbitrary, self-willed or domineering spirit, to counsel with the official brethren and with the church before doing anything of importance, to faithfully preach the Word, care for the wants of the membership, be an example in word and life to all the church and to be subject to the order of the general brotherhood in faith and practice, in all things, as defined by Annual Meeting.—"Classified Minutes", p 110, 111.

The office of deacon or "visiting brother", as he was described in 1835, is mentioned and his duties defined by the Annual meeting in that year, Art. 15. He was carefully subordinated to the ministry as a kind of *ordo minor.**

Both ministers and deacons were limited in their activity by their subordination to the church, the fountain of authority. Both classes were elected by the church and could be relieved of their offices by the church. Only the minister of the third degree, the elder, was ordained by the laying on of hands and prayer. In the course of the development there was great pressure brought to

*His duties are (1) to assist the ministers in making the annual visit to each member of the church to see whether he is in love and fellowship with all the members, or in case of division of the field for the purpose of that visit, or, in case the ministers are sick, he is to take the initiative in the visit in connection with whatever other brethren are deemed necessary; (2) to accompany the ministers to the investigation of any trouble in the church, or, provided it is not of special importance, to investigate it himself, when so required by the ministry of the church; (3) to oversee the poor of the church, visit the sick, to distribute money or grain to the needy and to keep a strict account of his receipts and expenditures on this account; (4) to bring anything he may hear of that demands attention to the notice of the ministry; (5) to assist ministers in the public worship by reading the Scripture and praying, and, in case no minister is present, to conduct the service, and to accompany a minister, if the latter requests it, to another district to hold meetings; and (6) to serve the tables at the Love Feasts, making all the necessary preparations for such occasions. In 1835, when this elaborate definition of duties was officially sanctioned the fifth (5) kind of duties was limited by the *caveat* that "it was the counsel of the old brethren that it is not their (the deacons') calling to rise to their feet in order to exhort". That is, it was thought best to confine their functions at public service, in the absence of a minister, to the conduct of the service, exclusive of the preaching, but if they did speak, they should do so sitting.—"Classified Minutes", p 95 f. In 1841 and 1843 he was further limited in this respect and in 1846 it was decided that a deacon has no right to appoint a meeting and preach, unless authorized by the church, but should confine himself to the duties for which he has been chosen. In 1871 it was decided that, when deacons spoke at all in meeting, they should do so standing. In 1846 it was decided that a deacon could not be ordained to the office of bishop.—"Classified Minutes", p 108.

bear upon the Meeting to have the other officers ordained likewise, but the demand for a visible incarnation of the unity of the church was too strong to permit the lesser officials to have the same treatment as the bishop of the Church.*

The relation of the ministry to its own and neighboring congregations gradually was defined. For example, as early as 1822 it was decided that an elder should not proceed to any course of action, without consulting the church. In 1849 it was decided that if the elder committed an error, he must confess to the church, like any other member. There was to be no chance for the growth of a hierarchy in that direction. The church was to be supreme. In 1879 it was decided that the ministry of the church, or all the officials together, have no authority to withhold a question of interest from the congregation. A minister has no authority, except in case of great danger that a congregation may depart from the order of the Church, to go into a neighboring congregation and meddle with its affairs, unless he be invited by the congregation or its elder. It was 1863 before this was clearly defined. The exception noted was made under the growth of the ideal of uniformity. In that case, however, the adjoining elders, not one elder alone, were to see that the congregation did not go astray.† This is an evidence that the seat of authority was being transferred from the local congregations to the Annual Meeting.

Thus, in the local church, the organization of the ministry developed from a formless one, in which there were ministers differing from one another only in natural abilities and age, to a ministry with three grades and a diaconate, each having clearly defined duties and reciprocal

*"Classified Minutes", p 95—112.
†"Classified Minutes", p 115, 116.

relations. The growth was from an undifferentiated to a differentiated ministry. The constitution of the local congregation had become complex.

As local churches grew strong and their territory broadened, it was found necessary to divide each one into several districts. In 1843 the decision was first made that each division constituted a separate church, even though one bishop might oversee them all, and that only the members of a particular district had the right to vote for ministers or deacons in that district.* Thus, the relations of congregations to each other were gradually assuming definiteness. The component society of the larger unit was developing.

In 1857 the relation of one congregation to another was more clearly defined by the ruling that no congregation has the right to interfere in the affairs of another by restoring "a member to his place in the church, when he had been excluded by another branch of the church, with out the concurrence of the church which excluded him".† In 1881 and 1882 the final step in the development of the local congregation was taken, when in consequence of the Old Order and Progressive divisions it was decided that in each congregation the portion that remained loyal to the ruling of Annual Meeting is the church, no matter how small a minority it may be. This was based on a decision of 1869 that a minority of a congregation may act with full authority in carrying out the decisions of Annual Meeting, "as the Annual Meeting is of higher authority than any one church".‡ There the process of unifying the organization became complete.

Beginning with 1788 there was developed by 1885 a

---

*"Classified Minutes", p 90.

†"Classified Minutes", p 55.

‡"Classified Minutes", p 57--60; Cf. "Revised Minutes", p 43, Art. 30, 1882.

complete theory of the relation of individual members to
the local congregation. At first the purpose of such definition was, to prevent immoral members from imposing
on a congregation that knew nothing about them, by re-
quiring them to present certificates from their home
church. The moving about that the expansion of the
Dunkers required accellerated this development, while
the conditions on which a certificate was granted became
ever more strict under the growing requirements of
church membership, owing to the development of the
rules of Annual Meeting known as "the order". In 1842
Annual Meeting decided that a local church has a right
to make resolutions, which if founded upon the Gospel,
are binding upon all the members. Who should say
whether they were according to the Gospel? Annual
Meeting. But in 1850, this apparent freedom of the local
church was limited by the ruling that "no district or
church has any right to make changes in anything whatsoever, contrary to ancient order, without proper investigation before, and the general consent of the Annual
Meeting. In 1863 it was decided that a- local congregation cannot "be congregational, or act independent from
the churches of our Fraternity, and still be in full union
with the church", "according to the Gospel and the order
of the Brethren".* Hence, the local church has authority over the individual member only when the church is
in submission to Annual Meeting–striking evidence of
the growth of the desire for unity.

In 1856 a proposal to form "districts of five, six or
more, adjoining churches, for the purpose of meeting
jointly at least once a year, settling difficulties, etc., and
thus lessening the business of our "Yearly Meeting",

*"Classified Minutes", p 54, 55.

was approved by Annual Meeting.* Not until 1866, however, had the church organization been so far developed that the Annual Meeting enacted a scheme of district organization called *District Meeting*. Then it was recommended "that each State form itself into convenient District Meetings", and the plan of organization was minutely described.† By this invention a complete scheme of church organization was formulated that changed the theory of the government in many respects. For example, it became impossible now to take questions directly from the local congregation to Annual Meeting as hitherto, except that any member who had fallen under the condemnation of the church might appeal to Annual Meeting by presenting a petition signed by a number of the members of the church.‡

Thus, with increasing membership and the growth of congregations, and with the growth of means of communication, the variations of doctrine and practice, that the years of isolation following the expansion had engendered, became apparent and demanded settlement under the growing ideal of unity. The District Meeting was an invention for the division of social labor. The invention was contingent upon the growth of the Dunkers numerically and upon the development of means of communica-

*"Classified Minutes", p 50.

†The Meeting was to be constituted by one or two representatives from each organized church. The style of procedure was to be as much like the ordinary council meeting of the local church as possible. Their duty was to settle questions of interest local to that district and thus assist Annual Meeting in the transaction of the increasing business. Hitherto all questions of merely local interest that could not be settled in the local congregation was carried to Annual Meeting. No business could come before District Meeting until it had first passed through the church in which it originated.

‡"Classified Minutes", p 13.

tion and the consequent development of dogmatic like-mindedness.

The process of socialization is illustrated best, perhaps, in the development of *the Annual Meeting*. Frequency of communication and association, growth of reflective sympathy and the rise of the ideals that dominated their thought led to the development. This tendency was furthered by the necessity of pronouncing upon questions of doctrine, of interpreting customs and of unifying diverse elements in the membership. Permanence of cooperation in Annual Meeting showed the wisdom of such a meeting for the exchange of views, for the settlement of local difficulties and for pronouncements on difficult questions, while the pleasures of the meeting also made for its continuance.

It may seem remarkable that no great development took place in this body until 1866. The committee, whose business it was to consider all matters presented and to decide what should come before the Meeting, and out of which body the Standing Committee was finally developed, suffered practically no change until 1868. Furthermore, the method of presenting queries to Annual Meeting is a survival from the time of its origin in 1742.

It would be a mistake, however, to suppose that there was no development until that late date. In minor matters many changes were made. In 1813 the necessity of having some from each church present at Annual Meeting found voice. In 1832 it was decided that the date of beginning the Meeting should be changed to Pentecost and that the opening service should be held on Sunday instead of Friday or Saturday as hitherto.* In 1848 it was recom-

---

*"Classified Minutes", p 7. The public preaching service and Love Feast occupied Sunday and the business sessions began on Monday. After much discussion in 1846 it was decided to go back to the plan of having the

mended that Monday following Whitsuntide should be observed "as a day of general fasting and prayer", hence the business did not begin until Tuesday. That is the present practice. Monday is now occupied with Educational, Sunday School and Missionary Meetings. In 1851 and 1855 it was decided that there should be no communion meeting in connection with the Annual Meeting, because of the great crowds in attendance.*

In 1813 the Annual Meeting was urging the overseers of the churches to advertise the time and place of holding it, so that more might attend. In 1847 the attendance had become so large that the meeting was made a delegate body, with the provision that "not more than two be sent from each church, with a written certificate, containing, also, the queries to be presented (by the church which they represent) to the Yearly Meeting."† Finally, in 1882 representation was placed on the basis of one delegate for each two hundred members, or fraction thereof, in a congregation, not to exceed two delegates from any congregation. While all members present might join in the discussion, all questions that did not pass by unanimous consent were to be decided by a two-thirds majority of the delegates present. Each member of the Standing Committee was counted as one delegate in this voting.

By equal strides, with the development in organization went the growth in the theory of the authority of the Annual Meeting. As early as 1805 we find a minute that says, "Further, it has been considered, that when there is made a conclusion at the big Yearly Meeting, and there

private business sessions on Friday and Saturday. Finally, in 1847 it was decided that the new plan of holding the business sessions, after the Sunday services, was best.

*"Classified Minutes", p 10, 1i.

†"Classified Minutes", p 8.

are members who would not heed, nor conduct themselves accordingly, it has been concluded unitedly, that when such persons cannot convince the Church by evidence from Holy Scripture, and would or did rise up against said Church conclusion, would not hear or obey at all, in such case we could not well do otherwise, but after sufficient and friendly admonition, set them back from the breaking of bread until they learn to do better and become obedient."* This is the penalty of suspension, not expulsion. In 1848 a query was sent up asking whether it would not be expedient to refer the decisions of Annual Meeting back to the congregations for final approval before they became binding, but it was decided "that it would not be expedient so to do, as it would be the means of accumulating the amount of business."† However, in 1850 it was decided that anyone not satisfied with a decision could, with the consent of his congregation, bring it before another Annual Meeting for reconsideration.

The stricter practice began with a decision in 1858 in regard to the case of *a private member*, who held the counsel of the Meeting in disrespect. It was decided that the individual should be admonished and, if he refused to hear, "should be dealt with according to Matt. xviii."‡ At that time the desire for unanimity had not yet become so controlling that the Meeting was willing to go any length to secure it, for in reply to a question as to whether a minister and some members of a congregation, who had violated the decisions of Annual Meeting, should "not fall into the hands of brethren of adjacent districts, as offenders, and to be dealt with as such," it was decid-

*"Classified Minutes", p 28.

†"Classified Minutes," p 28.

‡Ibid, p 29.

ed that the means already in use were "sufficient to give the teachers and housekeepers and members in general, the decisions of our Annual Council for the perfecting of love and union throughout the Brotherhood," that "the Gospel, with the practice, or order, consistent with the Gospel, will preserve the union of the Brotherhood."

In 1860 a further step towards the absolute authority of the Annual Meeting was taken in a decision in reply to the query, "Is it, then, consistent with our profession, (that the New Testament was their only rule of faith and practice), to make a strict observance of the Minutes of the Annual Council a test of fellowship?" The answer was, "The decisions of the Annual Meeting are obligatory until such decisions shall be repealed by the same authority". However, the Meeting was not yet prepared to stand by what was involved in that decision, as is shown by the answer to the query in 1865. "Does the Annual Council make laws, or give advice only, in cases where it has no direct Gospel on the subject?" The reply was, "It gives advice only." In the struggles with the increasing number of those who rebelled against the growing power of Annual Meeting the theory gradually assumed its final form. In 1871 it was decided to discipline brethren who spoke or wrote disrespectfully of the decisions of the Annual Meeting. The final step was taken in 1882, when the Annual Meeting granted a petition from some District Meeting "that hereafter all queries sent to Annual Meeting for decision, shall in all cases be decided according to the Scriptures, where there is anything direct ('Thus saith the Lord,') applying to the question. And all questions to which there is no direct *expressed Scripture* applying, shall be decided according to the spirit and meaning of the Scripture. And that decision shall be *mandatory* to all the churches having such cases as the decision covers. And all who shall not so *heed* and *observe* it, shall be held as not *hearing* the Church, and shall be dealt with accordingly."* The next year this was modified by the declaration that this "decision shall not be so construed as to prevent the Annual Meeting from giving advice when it deems it proper to do so, and that given as advice, shall be so entered upon the Minutes."† Thus, the theory of the authority of Annual Meeting had developed. At first its decisions were advice only. By 1882 its decisions were advice *only when such was plainly stated in the minutes,* all other decisions were "mandatory." The steps in that development were taken between 1865 and 1882. That was the period of rapid social development in the country at large and also of the rapid socialization of the Dunker church along other lines.

Even as constituted in Zinzendorf's Synods, the committee of control, out of which grew *the Standing Committee* in the Dunker church, was a device of no mean power. It had absolute control over what should come before the Synod. As it developed in the Dunker fraternity it became, in effect, *the church.* Step by step it evolved into an engine of tremendous power. At first, a means whereby trivial and local questions might be kept out of the meeting, a device for the saving of time, it became in the course of the history an instrument by which free discussion was stifled and the will of a small minority was impressed upon local churches all over the Brotherhood, even in cases when every member in that congregation rebelled against its procedure. This was possible because of its powers in two capacities—its right, to control queries, and its right to appoint committees to local churches.

*"Classified Minutes", p 31. (Italics theirs).
†"Classified Minutes," p 31.

The organization of the Standing Committee was outlined in 1866. According to that plan it was to be composed of ordained elders, chosen by the elders of the church where the Meeting was held, three from each of the States, Virginia, Maryland, Pennsylvania, Ohio, Indiana and Illinois, and two from each of the other states in which there were Dunker churches, except that whenever any state had ten bishops within it, it should be entitled to three members of the Committee. This plan was modified in 1868 by a decision that the members of the Standing Committee should be elected by the District Meetings, one elder from each district.*

Its officers, to be chosen by itself, were a moderator, a writing clerk, a reading clerk and a doorkeeper with duties appropriate to each. It was provided that the moderator of the Standing Committee should be the presiding officer of the Meeting. Two years later it was decided that the officers, except moderator, might be chosen from the members of the Annual Meeting who were not members of the Standing Committee. In 1880 it was decided that the Moderator also need not be chosen from the members of the Standing Committee. In 1871 there were protests against the assumption of authority by the Standing Committee and a recommendation was made that there be a frequent change in Moderators and clerks. In 1885 the Meeting decided "that no brother shall be allowed to serve with the Standing Committee as Moderator or Clerk more than twice in four years." Thus, gradually the organization of the Standing Committee was perfected.

The primary purpose of the Standing Committee originally was to serve as a committee of general arrangement for the Annual Meeting. The duties naturally fell into

*"Classified Minutes", p 14, 39.

two classes, the consideration of what queries should be presented to Annual Meeting and the arrangement of the place of meeting. In the course of time the two classes of duties were divorced and, while those relating to the matters to be presented to the Meeting were left in the hands of the Standing Committee, the other class was given into the hands of what came to be called the Committee of Arrangements, appointed by the local church where the meeting was held.

Perhaps as important as the duty of acting as a committee to consider queries beforehand and determine what should come before Annual Meeting was the duty of appointing committees to settle troubles in local churches. In case there was trouble in a congregation it early became the practice to ask help from either the elders living in an adjoining church, or of the Annual Meeting. The former was the earlier practice. As early as 1791 advice was given by visiting brethren to the Germantown church, but it was not a committee sent from Annual Meeting.* The earliest committee known to have been sent to settle trouble in a local church was in 1849.† The Standing Committee had the appointment of such committees. Gradually the practice of settling trouble in a congregation by a committee from Annual Meeting almost superseded the earlier method of calling in adjoining elders.‡ After the organization of District Meetings a local church could apply for a committee from the District instead of one from Annual Meeting.

*Brumbaugh, "History of the Brethren", p 504. Brumbaugh gives the reader the impression that this was a committee asked of Annual Meeting by the Germantown church. According to the record quoted it was rather a general meeting, perhaps the Annual Meeting for that year. On p 491 Brumbaugh seems to incline to that opinion himself.

†"Classified Minutes", p 388.

‡"Classified Minutes", p 41-45.

However, the authority of the committees sent by the latter had been advanced to such a degree by 1876 that a request was granted by Annual Meeting that the power of such committees be limited, "so as not to allow them to expel a majority of any church, unless their decision is ratified by the Annual Meeting in open session".* The climax of this development was reached during the troublous days of 1880-1882. After that the liberalization of the committee system, as also of the whole organization, began.

Thus did the Dunker church develop in organization and ideals, as it grew in numbers and as the United States increased in population and social integration. It had become practically socialized by 1880, with the exception of the last step in the process, liberalization, which is to be noticed in the next chapter. The ultimate cause of this process will be noticed after the development has been traced to its completion.

The hiatus in Dunker history between the close of the Revolutionary War and 1850 has often been noticed. The Dunker church went out into the wilderness at the beginning of that period, and shared in the development of the great Central Plain. She began to come to self-consciousness about 1835 and from that time on to 1882 worked ceaselessly at the task of unifying her organic structure, her practices and her beliefs. When in 1880 the Old Order Brethren withdrew and in 1882 the Progressive Brethren were expelled, the task was complete. It was unification by heroic methods, but it had the great merit of being effective. Another and greater task then awaited her.

*"Classified Minutes", p 48.

CHAPTER V.

Liberalization of the Dunkers.

The yearning of the Dunkers for unity was expressed most clearly in the "mandatory" decision of the Annual Meeting of 1882. While the passion for homogeneity and the consequent expulsion of "Progressives" continued at high tension for some time, it was not long before the Annual Meeting elders had either cowed into submission or expelled the troublesome element and homogeneity became relatively perfect. This had two results: it enabled the Church to devote its energies to the acquisition of members; and, as there was now a greater social homogeneity, there began the growth of greater liberty, both personal and associational, in social mind and social organization.

Great as was the increase of the Dunker population from 1790, when there was not more than 1462 members in America, to 1881-2, when there were 57,749, the increase from the latter date to the present was even more startling.* In 1890, the total number of Dunkers in the four bodies was 73,795, a gain of almost 28 per cent for the the nine years.† On Jan. 5, 1905, according to Dr. Carroll, there were 114,194, a gain in 25 years of more than 97.7 per cent.‡

It has often been a matter of surprise that such rapid increase in membership should have immediately followed a period of strife and heart-breaking such as was never known before in the history of the denomination.

*Howard Miller, "Record of the Faithful", p 66. At last after diligent search and some advertising this first official census of the Dunkers came into my hands and I am able to give statistics of the Dunkers just at the turning point of their recent and most striking history.

†U. S. Census, 1890.

‡"Christian Advocate", New York City.

When one looks at the matter, however, from the sociological point of view, he can easily understand it. Coming down from the period following the expansion were three main classes in the Dunker population.

There was the class composed of those that had been most isolated from the influences of an advancing civilization, who, by nature conservative, had not been touched by the social influences that were remaking society in the United States, and who stood like a rock against all changes from the old ways of their fathers. These were what came to be called the Old Order Brethren. Their stronghold numerically was in the Miami Valley of Ohio, although in almost every Dunker congregation in 1880 there were more or less of such.

Then there was the class at the other extreme, composed of members who had been most influenced by the extra-Dunker society. For the most part these were those who, naturally progressive, had lived in towns or cities, or in communities that were up-to-date socially. They had been affected by the social influences of a rapidly developing civilization. Many of them in their youth had attended the public schools in towns near their homes, had access to the newspapers, had acquired a taste for literature, and had learned that there were good people outside the Dunker church. In short, they were those who had been affected so far by the civilization about them that the Dunker ideas and customs that had no "thus saith the Lord" to support them had no standing in their estimation. Seeing the advantage of education to individuals and the church, they were in favor of higher schools and colleges. Realizing the benefits that the other churches were getting out of Sunday schools, prayer meetings and revival meetings, they advocated these institutions. Appreciating the necessity of having some organ for the discussion of questions of interest to the denomination and the dissemination of new ideas, they started the church papers. Believing that the only way for the church to succeed in the changing conditions of social life was to adapt the church in non-essentials to the age in which they lived, they advocated the adoption of modern methods of church work, modern ideas and customs. Their party was known as the Progressives.

Between these two classes, more numerous by far than both of the others together, was the third class, the Conservatives, as they were called. This party was composed of those that had been influenced by the environing society more than the Old Order Brethren, but less than the Progressives, and felt that time would bring about all the changes that were necessary. They were less logical than either of the other parties, and therefore could the more easily compromise. At first they favored keeping the church intact at almost any price, but, as the Progressives became more aggressive and radical, and as the men in control of the Annual Meeting were more favorable to the Old Order Brethren than to the Progressives, the Annual Meeting finally decided that the latter must get out, in order to save the Old Order Brethren to the church and for the sake of the dignity of the Annual Meeting.

The result of the trouble was that the Old Order Brethren withdrew, and the Progressives were expelled by thousands. Many thought that these ruptures in the Church would destroy it, and were surprised when all three branches prospered as never before. One has but to read the church papers of that day to realize the dark apprehensions that filled the mind of almost every writer on both sides.*

*Just one example will suffice. In 1881–1882 Howard Miller, one of the keenest-minded men in the Conservative party, wrote, "It is therefore safe

How is the growth to be explained? By the circumstance that this segregation of unlike elements in the Dunker church increased the homogeneity of each party, developed consciousness of kind very completely, precipitated conflict between the three parties and developed zeal in a corresponding degree. On the other hand the disappearance of the causes of friction in each body stopped the controversy, and gave each time to devote its energies to the building up of its membership. This increasing social homogeneity gave rise to greatly increased activity and, consequently, to a vast increase in numbers.

Another result of the segregation of the different social elements in the Dunker church was the liberty consequent on the social homogeneity in the conservative and progressive parties. Liberty of thought, custom and organization is possible only when the population has become socially homogeneous. As we saw in the previous chapter, it was the efforts of a predominant, homogeneous party to reduce the heterogeneity of the membership that led to the policy of coercion, against which the Progressives revolted. Therefore when the unlike social elements separated, policies of liberalization became possible in the progressive and conservative parties, because of the change that took place in the mode of likemindedness. Reverence for tradition had been characteristic of their type of mind. It now became more liberal. How this change in the type of mind took place must now be explained. Generally a change in the social mind is effected in two ways in the period following the time of consolidation in any society; (1) by the freeing of energies from the tasks of welding the society into a

to estimate the strength of the Brethren in the United States as above, and for many years to come, at our present rate of growth; 'between' 55,-000 and '60,000' will be a truthful statement of our strength."—"Record of the Faithful", p 87. Yet, in 1890, they had 73,795.

political unity by conflict and the devotion of those energies to the criticism of current thought, policy, customs,
and organization of the society, and (2) by the physical
and psychical plasticity consequent on the amalgamation
of different social elements. Following the Civil War
the social mind of the people of the United States was so
changed and became more liberal.

Only indirectly, however, was the social mind of the
smaller social unit, the Dunker church, affected by the
broadening influences that the soldiers brought back with
them from that war, for the Dunkers were a peace people
and did not participate in the struggle. Nevertheless,
an occasional Dunker's son had gone to the front. Perhaps, after his return he joined the Church and married,
possibly, a Dunker girl. More frequently a non-Dunker
who had been a soldier, did the same thing. In these
ways the Dunkers were touched to a certain extent by
the same influences that worked the change in the social
mind of the integral society. For the most part, however,
such change in the social mind of the Dunkers as was
due to the Civil War can be traced to the impression of
the ideals of the society about them upon the Dunkers,
and the imitation by the latter of the environing society.

More important than this indirect influence was the
condition within the Dunker church itself that made possible such a change. After the middle of the century,
and especially after the close of the Civil War, certain of
the Dunkers found themselves released from the more
serious part of the burdens incident to building homes
and clearing farms in the wilderness. Their energies
and money were freed for the purposes of culture. They
could now afford to devote time and money to the education of their children and could take a greater interest in

the affairs of the world, as these affairs were to be known through the medium of books and newspapers. Furthermore, these conditions also allowed time and energy to be devoted to the examination and criticism of the ideas, customs, policies and organization of the Dunker church itself by its members. Very significant is the fact that the first Dunker newspaper since Sauer's "Geistliche Magazin" was a small monthy that originated at Poland, Ohio, in 1851. And still more significant was the fact that thirteen years later the "Christian Family Companion", a weekly, edited and published by Henry R. Holsinger, found a large number of readers in the Dunker church, for it was avowedly progressive in its tendencies, and devoted much space to the criticism of the Church.* The fact that it leaped into popularity so quickly shows that Dunkers were in the mood to criticise their church.

This freedom from the demands of home-making not only freed Dunker energy to be devoted to criticism of the church, but it also permitted their children to have a broader experience and culture. Their homes were built, their farms were bringing them comfortable returns, there was a great increase of social advantages for their children in the rapidly growing towns about them. Schools were growing up rapidly and, since there was not now a need for all the children on the farm, some of them, generally the younger ones, were sent to school at the nearby town. This circumstance made the social mind of such more plastic. After imitating the culture of the extra-Dunker society, such a child went back home carrying the broader outlook obtained in the town, thus affecting in some measure the social mind of the family to

*See especially Holsinger, "History of the Tunkers, etc.", p 470 f. As he was the leader of the Progressives and the advocate of most of the changes that took place the importance of his book for this period cannot be exaggerated. Cf. Howard Miller, "Record of the Faithful", p 89 f.

which such a youth belonged, and having a most potent influence on the social mind of the next generation.*

Therefore, when these young men began to advocate their views through such papers as the "Christian Family Companion", and the "Progressive Christian", the latter paper started in Berlin, Penna., by Holsinger and Beer in 1878, a process of conflict began within the church. Two tendencies were pitted against each other: the tendency towards consolidation and uniformity, backed by the likemindedness of the great majority of the church, and the tendency towards liberalization and progress, supported by the small but aggressive party

---

*That such was the process by which the social mind of the Dunkers was liberalized is shown by the case of Henry R. Holsinger, to whom more than to any other man in the Dunker fraternity is due the credit of bringing about the liberal epoch in that church. His father was a better educated man than most of the Dunker preachers of that day. "He was about the only English-speaking Tunker in the community".—Holsinger, "History of the Tunkers, etc.", p 340. He was a lover of poetry and "could recite page after page from many of the poets". Holsinger testifies that while he never succeeded in getting more than a common school education, he himself always had a deep yearning for an education. Brought up in such a family that desire was but natural. He was not afraid of Sunday schools, and from the very first his type of mind was rational rather than dogmatic. In his early manhood he served a year's apprenticeship in the printing office of the "Gospel Visitor", the first Dunker paper in the nineteenth century, and by travel and reading became more than ever convinced that there were many things in the Dunker church that must be changed. He felt the influence of the thought of the world about him, and saw the contrast between the Dunker preachers, ideas, culture, customs and organization and those of the other churches of the country. He felt the influence of the new social era that had dawned upon the United States and endeavored to impress what he felt upon the Dunker church.

Holsinger's case is typical, for in the Dunker church there were many young men who had duplicated his experience by imitating the broader culture of the growing American social life. Much the same broadening influences had surrounded Henry Kurtz, the founder of the first modern Dunker paper.—Holsinger, "History of the Tunkers, etc.", p 3-8, 339 f, 350 f, 354, 470 f.

composed of men that had been affected by the more
rational social mind of American society.

The final sifting, however, did not occur until the
the divisions were made in 1880-1882. Then a process of social selection began. The ultra-conservatives
in the Dunker church either modified their views or
went with the Old Order Brethren. The extreme progressives, in like manner, went out with Holsinger
and the Progressives. This process continued for years,
until gradually the more progressive members were to be
found in the Brethren church, as the progressives called
themselves, the ultra-conservatives in the Old Order
Brethren church, while the moderates of both tendencies
remained with the moderately conservative party known
officially as the German Baptist Brethren.

The effect of the cessation of strife and the social homogeneity, consequent upon this social selection, was
marked on the social mind of each of the parties. At
once, all incentives to progress were inhibited in the case
of the Old Order Brethren. They were so homogeneous
that liberalization was impossible.

Among the Progressives, there was sufficient heterogeneity to insure the continuance of the development of
the social mind, while there was also a tendency to
become less radical than it seemed at first they might
become.

The Conservatives, on the other hand, retained a large
number of members progressively inclined, who at once
began to criticise and reconstruct the Dunker church,
which tendency was furthered by the necessity of so
liberalizing the church as to prevent more of the progressively inclined from going over to the Progressives.

On the last two parties it had the effect of freeing
energies, long wasted in controversy, for purposes of crit-

icism, reconstruction and aggressive measures for increasing the membership. Thus, it reacted upon the social population and gave the Dunker church, especially in the two largest branches, the great increase in membership noted above.

Finally, this social selection reacted also upon the individuals composing the membership of each party. The conservative became more liberal and that insured that the members of the middle party should become constantly more progressive, because progress is possible only when there is social heterogeneity that is of such degree that it is constantly becoming more homogeneous.* Both the Progressives and Conservatives, the latter only slightly less than the former, now learned to value rational more than formal likemindedness.

In the period when society is becoming unified, measures of coercion are necessary. One of the first things, however, that a society whose membership has become homogeneous and whose social mind has become rational rather than formal has to do is to liberalize its organization. With the change described above in the type of likemindedness of the Dunker church there went this change in the organization. In the period previous to 1882 the power of the organization had rested practically in the hands of the Standing Committee, although theoretically in the Annual Meeting, not in the membership of the church in the congregations. There was no appeal to right and legality as a higher law than the law of the Scriptures as interpreted by the traditions of the fathers. In the present period, however, the conceptions of a law that was higher than the tradition began to appear. The conception of legality began to arise. This conception originated in the minds of the Progressives

*Giddings, "Democracy and Empire", p. 53.

and their sympathizers among the Conservatives in the struggle of 1882, when Henry R. Holsinger was expelled from the church by the Annual Meeting.* Thus, in both branches a conception of a law above the will of the majority, arose in the minds of many of the Dunkers. After their separation this idea continued to develop.

Immediately on the organization of the Progressives they provided that their organization should have a care for the safe-guarding of the rights of the individual against the arbitrary power of the few, and thus gave expression to their regard for a legality and justice that is above the traditions of the church.†

Among the Conservatives the progress towards legality has been slower, but it has been none the less real. The Annual Meeting has never given expression to this conception in any decision, but in practice it has admitted it, ever since shortly after the organization of the Progressives as a separate body. To have continued the former arbitrary and coercive policy would have driven thousands of their members into the progressive branch of the church.

That the date 1882 is only approximately correct as the dividing point between the period of centralization and the period of liberalization in the Dunker church is indicated by nothing so clearly as by the growth, within the church, of voluntary associations, such as colleges, newspapers, missionary societies and old folks' homes. These voluntary organizations had begun with the rise of the first newspaper, the "Gospel Visitor," which was author-

---

*See remarks of D. C. Moomaw, Landon West, Robert H. Miller, etc., Holsinger, "History of the Tunkers", p 515-525.

†See "Declaration of Principles", in Holsinger, "History of the Tunkers, etc.", p 530 f.

ized by the Annual Meeting in 1851.* Between that time and 1882 no less than 14 papers, devoted to the discussion of church or Sunday school questions, and representing different tendencies in the fraternity, arose in the Dunker church.†

Moreover, at the time of the division in the Dunker organization in 1882, there had been organized four colleges, one each in Virginia, Pennsylvania. Ohio and Illinois. The Huntington Normal College at Huntington, Penna., started in 1876, was the first of these, although there had been several abortive attempts made to organize Dunker schools, the first by Jacob Miller in 1852 in Pennsylvania.‡ Thus, the liberal era in the Dunker church really began about 1850, but did not become dominant in the church until after 1882. From that time on the social constitution of the Dunker church, in both its leading branches, became more complex. Organizations of all kinds multiplied. Among the Conservatives, since that time at least four more colleges have been started, two more periodicals have been begun, while the publishing interests of that branch have become so prosperous that each year there is about $10,000 in profits to be devoted to the missionary work of that church.

Before that date, the Dunker church had a small mission in Denmark, but city and foreign mission work in

---

*"Considered, at this Council, that we will not forbid Bro. Henry Kurtz to go on with the paper for one year; and that all the brethren or churches will impartially examine the *Gospel Visitor*, and if found wrong or injurious, let them send in their objections at the next Annual Meeting." In 1853 is found the last reference to this paper, as follows: "In regard to the fourth query of last year's minutes, concerning the *Gospel Visitor?* Inasmuch as the *Visitor* is a private undertaking of its editor, we unanimously conclude that this Meeting should not any further interfere with it."—"Classified Minutes", p 323, 324.

†All were published in English, except a small one in German.

‡Holsinger, "History of the Tunkers, etc.," p 365.

general was frowned upon. Following the division in
1882, the General Missionary and Tract Committee, was
organized. This does successful work in a number of
large cities, has missions in India, Switzerland, Sweden,
Denmark and France. Since then has originated the Educational, Sunday School and Missionary Meetings held
in connection with the Annual Meeting.

Subsequent to the division of the Dunker church occurred the great development in the social constitution
of the local congregation. The organization of Sunday
schools began previous to that time but by far the greater
number have been organized since. Young peoples' societies and ladies' aid societies have originated since 1882,
as well as local mission bands. Thus, the social constitution of the Conservative branch of the Dunker church
has been subsequent, and also consequent, to the liberalization of the social mind of the Dunkers. As appreciation of the value of variety in their society grew, the
social constitution developed.*

The danger of losing members by their going to the
Progressives, forced the Conservatives, shortly after the
division of the church in 1882, to stop short in their coercion of the individual in the interest of uniformity and
to allow him more liberty of action. As the coercion had
been limited almost entirely to securing uniformity in
matters described by the phrase "the order of the
church", which pertained largely to dress and customs,
naturally the liberty allowed was on this point. Individual initiative henceforth was allowed a greater place.

The whole church was so affected by this change in the
social mind that entirely new policies were adopted.

Instead of meeting with suspicion those who tried to
introduce a wider culture and warning them that they

*Giddings, "Inductive Sociology", p 224.

were departing from the ways of the fathers, the church authorities and the moulders of thought encouraged them. Perhaps, the most striking policy that was now inaugurated was that of encouraging a wider intercourse with the world, to which they had so long been strangers. One of their foremost men, D. L. Miller, made several journeys around the world visiting the places of interest and writing of them in the denominational paper, the *Gospel Messenger.* The articles were published later in book form. That the church as a whole was animated by a new spirit is shown by the fact that his articles were the most popular of any in the paper and that his books enjoyed, and still enjoy, a phenomenal sale.

Another result of this new phase of the social mind was the fact that the schools of the church were not only encouraged, but were thronged with Dunker students. Educationally, the Dunker church's horizon was not bounded by its own schools. The graduates of these were encouraged to seek the best universities of this country and Europe. The increase of books and magazines in Dunker homes and the demands by Dunker congregations in many places, especially in the cities, for educated preachers bore witness to the rapid change that had come over the policies of the Dunker church. While it never has avowed a policy to extend its intercourse with the world about it and to be in favor of free investigation, the Dunker church has practically adopted the policy of world-wide intercourse. Consequently modern means of communication, such as the rural mail delivery, the daily newspaper, the telephone and the illustrated and scientific magazine, have been eagerly adopted by most of the Dunker people.* The fact that one of the most en-

*In 1905 the Annual Meeting of the Old Order Brethren, the ultra-conservative party, decided against telephones.

lightened Dunkers, Dr. M. G. Brumbaugh, of the University of Pennsylvania, could criticise the Dunker church in his "History of the Brethren", in 1899, and yet enjoy the confidence of the church and that his books sold among the Dunkers by the thousands shows that the policy of harking back to tradition has given place to that of free investigation.*

Lastly, a policy of legality has displaced to a certain extent the policy of arbitrary exercise of power in the conduct of the Annual Meeting, and in the conduct of trials of members in most congregations.

The liberalization of the Dunker church, however, is not yet complete. As the process began before the division in 1882, so the policy of coercion did not cease altogether at that date. These periods overlap each other. While, on the whole, liberal policies, and rational sentiments dominate the Dunker church today, all the respect for tradition and all coercion upon the individual has not ceased. But the Dunker church has achieved a social organization that maintains essential unity and is stronger than it ever was, while, at the same time, it allows a greater measure of individual and social liberty than ever before. Those are the marks of a progressive and liberal society.

Furthermore, in the Dunker church have appeared the beginnings of the third stage of social evolution, sociocracy, by which is meant the stage in the development of a constituent society which corresponds to democracy in an integral society.

This was brought about by the same causes in both cases. The liberal stage gave rise to individual initiative and allowed the Dunkers to adopt the best methods of organization, the best inventions both in their church work

*"History of the Brethren", p 505 f. 526, 539, 543, 546 f.

and in their homes and business. That gave rise to increase of the Dunker wealth and also Dunker population. The liberalization of the Dunker organization, the broadening of the Dunker mind with the consequent modification of Dunker customs, thought and policies, resulted in a great increase in the membership apart from natural growth. It made possible a successful appeal to people that had not been raised Dunkers and this led to complexity of the Dunker membership. This process is still going on.

Social selection is at work on the Dunker population, determining the physical and psychical classes and thus preparing for a further development of the social mind. The Dunker church has not reached the stage of social development represented by American society as a whole, but under the influence both of the environing society and also of causes operating within itself, it is rapidly evolving toward such a stage.

CHAPTER VI.

PRESENT CONDITIONS IN THE DUNKER CHURCH.

1. *Numbers.*

In 1770 there were fifteen congregations of Dunkers in Pennsylvania, with a membership of 663, one in New Jersey with 46 members, a total of 709 members in sixteen congregations. If the seventeen churches in Maryland and the other southern colonies had as high an average membership as these, which is hardly likely, since they were newer congregations, than in 1790 there were not more than 1462 members in the territory now included in the United States.*

It would be interesting to know the number of Dunkers in different parts of the country during the period between the Revolutionary War and 1880, but there was no census of the Dunkers, until 1880, when Howard Miller was appointed to prepare one. His results together with all other available information is gathered together in the following table. It shows the entire Dunker population in 1880 and 1890, the numbers and distribution of the Progressives in 1905, and gives an indication of the distribution of the Conservatives in that year.

Numbers and geographical Distribution of the Dunker Population in the United States:

States	United States Census of 1890	Howard Miller's Census of 1880 in "Record of the Faithful", p 64.	†Progressives, "Statistical Report", 1905, by Mrs. A. H. Lichty	Conservatives, Number of *Gospel Messengers* taken in April, 1905.‡
Alabama................	....	....		20
Alaska	....	....	....	

*Morgan Edwards, "Materials towards a History of the Baptists in Jersey", p 385 f.

†Canada has 12 members. The Report is unpublished.

‡See, *Gospel Messenger*, April 29, 1905.

Arizona...............	....	....	20
Arkansas,	82,	20,	....	64
California,	290,	211,	310,	387
Colorado,	127,	80,	....	182
Connecticut...........	....	....	....
Delaware......	....	....	. ...
District of			
Columbia....	....	88,	67
Forida	41,	....	....	19
Georgia...............	....	....	2
Idaho,	40,	....	....	201
Illinois,	4,119,	4,407,	686,	1,532
Indiana,	12,350,	10,237,	3,275,	3,148
Indian Territory,	27,	....	....	27
Iowa,	3,470,	3,056,	841,	1,221
Kansas,	4,067,	2,358,	615,	1,459
Kentucky,	13,	....	....	5
Louisiana,	17,	.. ..	....	41
Maine.................	....	....	1
Maryland,	2,964,	2,604,	550,	843
Massachusetts	....	....	1
Michigan,	844,	659,	220,	326
Minnesota,	104,	129,	....	160
Mississippi............	....	....	4
Missouri,	2,090,	1,309,	12,	653
Montana	....	....	16
Nebraska,	1,441,	620,	439,	444
Nevada...............	....	....	1
New Hampshire.......	....	....	....
New Jersey,	191,	302,	101,	24
New Mexico....	....	....	1
New York............	....	....	43
North Carolina,	525,	288,	....	96
North Dakota....	....	9,	411
Ohio,	11,798,	9,362	2,443,	2,814
Oklahoma,	46,	....	....	296
Oregon,	280,	200,	....	191
Pennsylvania,	16,707,	14,557,	3,357,	4,058
Rhode Island.........	....	....	....
South Carolina.......	....	....	12
South Dakota,	102,	....	....	8
Tennessee,	1,249,	1,088,	12,	212

Texas,	95,	12,	....	96
Utah..............	....	....		2
Vermont..........	....	....		1
Virginia,	7,244,	4,965,	880,	1819
Washington,	26,	....	97,	185
West Virginia,	3,216,	1,587,	180,	473
Wisconsin,	199,	....	....	71
Wyoming,	21,	....	....	4
Total	73,795,	59,749,	14,117,	

Dr. Carroll, in his "Statistics of the Churches" published in the *Christian Advocate*, January 5, 1905 presents the following table:

Dunkards	Ministers	Churches	Communicants
1. Conservatives,	2,775	900	95,000
2. Old Order,	213	75	4,000
3. Progressives	265	144	15,000
4. Seventh Day (German)	5	6	194
Total	3,258	1,125	114,194

This summary is a relatively close estimate based upon reports sent in by the Conservatives. It throws no light on the distribution of the Dunkers. It is valuable only for the light it throws upon the relative strength of the four branches.

In 1890 there was a total membership in the four branches of 73,795 in 989 organizations. Compared with the estimate of their numbers a century before, this shows a rapid increase of membership. It also shows that, whereas the average size of a congregation in 1780 was 44 ⅓ members, in 1890 the average was 74 ⅔. In 1905, according to Dr. Carroll's figures, the average congregation had increased to 101 ½ members.

A glance over the combined table given above shows where growth has been vigorous. The states in which were the greatest numbers of Dunkers in 1890 were Pennsylvania, 16,707; Indiana, 12,350; Ohio, 11,798; Vir-

ginia, 7,244; Illinois, 4,119; Kansas, 4,067; Iowa, 3,470.
Perhaps the most striking thing that the table shows is
the remarkable increase since 1880. The phenomena of
of this period in the history of the Dunker church corresponds with the phenomena that are found in the history of nations in the period of civilization that follows
the development from the military-religious stage into
the liberal-legal.* In both cases the period is marked by
a great increase in population and a very pronounced
development in culture and organization.

2. *The Social Mind of the Dunkers.*

To the stimulus of economic opportunity and of political and religious freedom in America, the Dunkers responded in much the same way as their German fellows
of like faith, the Mennonites. Likewise, the newer portions of America at a later time presented the economic
opportunities that drew the Dunkers thither very early
and in great numbers. Today the Dunkers are like their
ancestors in their ready response to the stimulus of economic advantages. They are practical men, farmers for
the most part, ever alive to their business interests, and
quick to seize any new opportunity offered.

Among themselves mental and practiced resemblance
is very highly developed.

Their appreciation is keen in all matters that pertain
to agriculture, and less keen in affairs that do not touch
their immediate interests. Thus, in agriculture and
stock raising they are alive to the greatest discoveries.
They buy the best and most improved machinery, take
the latest and best farm papers, and attend the county
and state fairs in order to keep abreast with all that is
best in the world in which they are concerned. In matters of education and science, they are content with

*Giddings, "Elements of Sociology", p 290 f.

theories that have been outgrown for almost a century.
Within the last ten years, however, there has begun a
veritable renaissance among them. Many of their young
men have been seized with a great passion for education,
new theories of the universe have been finding adherents
among them. A new world has been opened up to them
through such men as D. L. Miller with his books on
travel, and M. G. Brumbaugh with his modern theories
of education. Their appreciation of the great world in
which they live has been cultivated by their contact with
the other social elements in a society that has gradually
been growing more cultured and liberal. Travel, schools,
good books, periodicals and all the influences of modern
American civilization have destroyed in a measure their
isolation, widened their experience, and developed their
appreciation.*

As farmers and business men the Dunkers have ever
been what are termed practical men. That mode of
practical activity known as utilization has been very
highly developed. They possess the skill of thirty five
generations of practice in farming. Their patient persistence, combined with skill and frugality, conquered the
wilderness, wherever they settled, and has earned them
the reputation of being the best farmers in the world.†
Among the Dunker farmers, there is less poverty than
among the members of any other denominations of Christians, unless it be among the Mennonites, themselves
German farmers.

Moreover, in their religion they have been nothing, if
not practical. Their religion has to do with ecclesiastical
policies and personal ethics, not with theology. Pietism

---

*Cf. the discussions in the *Gospel Messenger* in 1885, for example, with
those in the same paper in 1905.

†Kuhns, "German and Swiss Settlements of Colonial Pennsylvania", p 85.

has ever been practical activity rather than dogmatics. The Dunkers in this particular are true to their pietistic origin.

The Dunker type of disposition should probably be called domineering. This type of disposition reveals itself in the reverence that is required to be paid to the older members, to the governing officials of the congregation, and to any authority whatsoever, either in church or state, which does not oppress them in matters of conscience. The old man, the wealthy man, the successful man has always been reverenced among them. When once the church has spoken in the Annual Meeting, it becomes the duty of every member to render obedience to the decision. When a local congregation has expressed its mind on a matter, it is in bad taste, to say the least, for anyone to question the result. This disposition has played a large part in the history of the denomination. It made possible the imposition of the policy of coercion upon so large a part of the Dunker body for so long a time. It determined the sort of leaders that the Dunker church has produced,—men of the domineering type, who ruled by coercion rather than by their superior mental and moral qualities.*

Deeply religious, the Dunkers are not of the rationally conscientious, but rather of the austere, type of character. All their history has been a protest against the evils they saw in the great churches about them. They have

*See Holsinger, "History of the Tunkers, etc.'", p 473 f. The principle set forth in Matthew 18:17, "And if he (a brother in the church, who has wronged you) will not hear the church, let him be unto thee as a heathen man and a publican", has been the controlling principle in the thought of the Dunker church, as to how a man should be "dealt with" after the highest authority has spoken. That that is the last word, and that its use is very frequent is shown by a glance over the pages of the minutes of the Annual Meeting. The phrase, "let him be dealt with according to Matthew 18:17" occurs so often that it becomes wearisome.

always been opposed to worldly forms of amusement, and
have considered themselves a reforming party in Protestant Christianity.   They opposed slavery, and have
taken advanced ground on intemperance and the use of
tobacco.* All the Minutes of the Annual Meeting on
practical piety show the austere type of character.   In
the Dunkers today we find the same persistence and the
same faithfulness to what they conceive to be duty
as characterized their forbears of the eighteenth century.   Among new and hostile surroundings, but protected by social isolation, they have clung to their beliefs, in
spite of the sneers of other Christian denominations.

*These examples from the minutes of their Annual Meetihg, cast an in-
teresting light upon their attitude:

"Art. 2, 1781.—Concerning distilleries, we heartily counsel all brethren,
who have distilleries, that they should by all means endeavor to put them
away, in order to escape from the evil so often arising from them, and to
avoid offence, and in this the brethren are still entirely united with the
conclusion made at Pipe Creek, three years ago."

"Art. 12, 1895.—We the brethren of Beaver Creek congregation, petition
Annual Meeting through District Meeting of Western Maryland, to say
what shall be done in case a brother is appointed to act as gauger, or store-
keeper at a distillery, and has been requested to resign, but refuses to re-
linquish his office? Ans.—If the brother refuses to resign, he shall be dealt
with according to Matt. 18:17. See Eph. 5:11 and 1 Thess. 5:22." These
are only two of a number of decisions relating to the liquor traffic from 1778,
the Minutes of which year is the earliest we possess, down to the present
time.

Their position on tobacco is well indicated by the following decision of
the Annual Meeting:

"Art. 1, 1817.—Concerning the use of tobacco, it was in union considered,
that if a member should be contaminated with it, such should be admonished
to quit it; and if he would not be told, such a member could not be elected to
any office in the church."

"Art. 7, 1896.—(Salem Church, Southern District of Ohio).   We petition
Annual Meeting through District Meeting, to reconsider Art. 10 of Minutes
of Annual Meeting of 1889, and so amend, that no delegate to Annual Meeting or to District Meeting, or member of the Standing Committee, be accepted as such, who uses, raises, buys or sells tobacco.   Ans.—We grant
petition asked for."—"Classified Minutes," p 284, 285, 297; "Revised Minutes," p 158 f, 163 f.

In type of mind the Dunkers are dogmatic-emotional. They have held themselves so strictly to their ideas, and have been so earnest with their convictions that they have been intolerant of others. This has gone to such lengths that many of them believe that theirs is the only true church of Christ. This is not often asserted in so bold a fashion, and directly confronted with the question, they generally hedge.* They are driven to that position by the logic of their beliefs. With them, reasoning in maters religious, has been habitually deductive.

This type of mind, in connection with their austere type of character has produced martyrs among them. As a single example, Christopher Sauer, the Germantown printer, allowed himself to be despoiled of all his property, which was considerable for that day, and to be dubbed a traitor to the country, because he could not take the oath of allegiance to the new state of Pennsylvania, at the close of the Revolutionary War.† It was not because he was opposed to the state, or because he was a

---

*This attitude has been characteristic of them from the very first. Thus, when Gruber put the question squarely to Mack in Germany in the first years of the history of the sect, "How shall we know, beyond all doubt, that your new denomination, above all others, is to be recognized as the true church?", Mack answered, "We have no new denomination and no new ordinances, but simply desire to live in the old church which Christ established through the virtue of his own blood, and obey the commandment which was from the beginning; and it is not our desire to appear before men as the only established church of Christ; but we do anxiously desire to show forth undaunted godliness by the grace and power of Christ, as it was in Christ himself and in the church at Jerusalem. And, if we can succeed in setting forth the institutions of Christ and of the original church in a godly life and by holy conversations, and in keeping his ordinances, it appears to us that that should be sufficient to show to all men that we are the true church of Christ, But whosoever cannot recognize Christ in the holiness of his commandments would not be able to recognize the church of Christ, even if the twelve apostles were among them.—Holsinger, "History of the Tunkers, etc.", p 70; Cf. "Classified Minutes", *passim*.

†See "Colonial Records", Index, "Christopher Sauer."

Tory at heart, but because he was conscientiously opposed to taking an oath. It is this type of mind, with its accompanying disposition and character, that has had much to do in bringing this eighteenth century sect of Christians down into the twentieth century, not enfeebled, like the Quakers, but strong and vigorous, and, so far as one can see, with a future before them.

Before they left Germany, consciousness of kind among the Dunkers had become a strong affection for those of experiences and sentiments like their own. Their common sufferings and their organization prompted its further development. In Germantown the process was repeated. Their history in America has further developed their consciousness of kind. Today, having acted from common purposes so long under a closely unified organization, consciousness of kind is more highly developed than among any other religious body of which I know. It extends even to economic affairs. In any Dunker community it always pays the merchant to secure some Dunker to clerk in his store, in order to draw Dunker trade. It extends even to the various bodies of the Dunker body. There is more of the consciousness of kind among the various kinds of Dunkers than there is among Dunkers and non-Dunkers, of whatsoever race or religion. To be known as a member of any branch of the Dunker church is of great advantage today to merchants that desire Dunker trade. There is a large mail-order house, for example, in one of our large cities that gets most of the mail-order business of the Dunkers, simply because some of the proprietors are Dunkers. Moreover, any project in which Dunkers are interested, or which they recommend, is sure to secure the patronage of the Dunkers. Such enterprises

as farm colonies, investment companies, mines and manufacturing concerns are examples.

Through the control of so strong a consciousness of
kind, and through the moulding influences both of similar physical and social stimuli, and of intimate acquaintance and association, continued for so long a period, the
Dunkers have learned to will the same things and to act
together.

Nothing can illustrate the Dunker type of mind so well
as a survey of the present state of culture among them,
and the doctrines that are binding upon them today.

Education.

For many years after their arrival in this country the
Dunkers cared little about education. The Germantown
congregation were in a degree an exception, and it appears that Christopher Sauer and his son, Christopher,
Jr., made the exception. The elder Sauer was a university man in Germany, a graduate of Marburg.* It is
true that Mack and Beissel were interested in literary
work of the religious sort, but they were self-taught and
only by accommodation of language could they be called
educated men. It is true that in their time the common
people of Germany had a wider access to the sources of
knowledge than they had before the Reformation. Furthermore, the sectarianism of their age made necessary
a kind of education in dialectics and church history, but
like most of the information that a man "picks up", it
was not an ordered knowledge. Moreover, the quickening of the intellectual life, characteristic of the post-
Reformation period was not shared by the Dunkers to a
very great degree. Mack and Hochmann, together with
others, had edited the Berleberg Bible. Sauer set up in
1738, the first printing press in America to print in Ger-

*Brumbaugh, "History of the Brethren", p 345.

man, and thereby created opportunity for the development of literary activity of a sort amongst the Dunkers of Germantown. He himself wrote the copy for most of his publications. Alexander Mack, Jr., was a famous hymn writer, as well as the author of many polemical works in defence of Dunker doctrines. Beissel and many of his fellow members at Ephrata wrote German hymns, besides other kinds of religious literature, and about 1745 they had established a press. Yet it cannot be said that the early Dunkers favored education.

To Christopher Sauer, Jr., however, belongs the honor, so far as the Dunkers are concerned, of promoting high schools in the early days. In 1759 he helped to raise money for the building of the Germantown Academy, and was one of its trustees for many years. He was twice chosen president of the board. His father was opposed to an educated ministry.*

Beissel's Community took steps to provide instruction for the young of the vicinity at a time when no schools existed in that part of the wilderness. The "Chronicon Ephratense" says that many families in Philadelphia and other colonial cities sent their children to Ephrata to be educated. In 1748 Ludwig Hoecker, who, after the revival at Germantown had left the Germantown Dunkers and joined Beissel's Community, started a Sabbath school, with a purpose similar to that which later on moved Robert Raikes in England to open a Sunday school, the purpose being to instruct the young in the elementary branches of learning. This school was continued until the battle of Brandywine, in the Revolutionary War, when the room was taken for hospital services. It was never opened afterwards. Peter Miller, the successor of Beissel at Ephrata, was a university man from Germany, and the

*Brumbaugh, *loc. cit.*, p 251, 411; Sauer's "Almanacs", *passim.*

most learned man in the Province in his time. He gave impetus to the religious-literary activity at Ephrata. Nevertheless, when the story of this activity is all told, all is told about education in the Dunker church for almost a hundred years. The emphasis of general opinion among the Dunkers was all on the foolishness of human learning.*

Holsinger tells us that already in 1850 the movement had been started by a few friends of education in the church. It gained momentum through the following years, in the manner already described in Chapter V, in spite of the adverse decisions of the Annual meeting. Today there are within the Dunker church at least seven schools and colleges of a higher order than the public grammer schools, besides the one in the progressive branch.†

---

*"Classified Minutes", p 299-301.—Here is the first decision to be found among the published Minutes of the Annual Meeting on the subject of education. It is from the year 1831: "Whether it was considered advisable for a member to have his son educated in a college? Considered not advisable, inasmuch as experience has taught that such very seldom will come back afterwards to the humble ways of the Lord". Here is one in reference to high schools, from the year 1852: "How is it considered by brethren, if brethren aid and assist in building great houses for high schools, and send their children to the same? Considered that brethren should be very cautious and not mind high things but condescend to men of low estate. Rom. 12:15".

Finally, one from 1857: "What are the views of the present Annual Council in regard to the contemplated school, that was alluded to some time since in the Gospel Visitor? Ans.—It is conforming to the world. The Apostle Paul says: 'Knowledge puffeth up, but charity edifieth'".

†These seven are as follows: Huntington Normal School, Huntington, Penn., 1875, now Juniata College; McPherson College, McPherson, Kans., 1877; Ashland College, Ashland, Ohio, 1878, which is now owned by the Progressives; Mt. Morris College, Mt. Morris, Ill., 1879; Bridgewater College, Bridgewater, Va., 1830; Lordsburg College, Lordsburg, Calif., 1891; Plattsburg College, Plattsburg, Mo., 1897; North Manchester College, North Manchester, Ind., 1895.

The men that favored colleges a generation ago were those who, from 1870 on, gave the denomination much trouble by their stand on the question of dress and on the nature of the decisions of the Annual Meeting. After the crisis was passed in 1882, when the Old Order Brethren and the Progressives left the church, the Conservatives did nothing further towards buying or building new colleges until 1891. By that time the church had finished her reorganization, made necessary by the struggle through which she had gone, and from that time to the present the educational movement in general has been gaining much headway among the Dunker people. The movement is one indication of the change that is slowly but surely taking place in the type of mind among the Dunkers.

Throwing an interesting side light upon the Dunker type of mind is the fact that from Christopher Sauer, Jr. and Alexander Mack, Jr., to the end of the nineteenth century, the Dunker church did not produce one man of commanding genius, or one that contributed in any remarkable way to the thought or welfare of the nation. Good men she produced in great numbers, but of men with breadth of vision, of national, to say nothing of world-wide sympathy, or, of far-seeing constructive ability, there is no sign, until the times of men now living. But within the last twenty-five years, men of considerable promise have appeared among them. Two of the most prominent among these are D. L. Miller, author and traveler, to whose wise foresight and splendid devotion is due much of the success of the church in the last quarter of a century, and M. G. Brumbaugh, Professor of Pedagogy in the University of Pennsylvania, who is prominent in educational circles in Pennsylvania. These two are modern men in the best sense of the term. There are an increasing number among the Dunkers that have had the advantages of the best university education in this country and a few that have taken degrees in Europe.

The progressive branch has been occupied with the work of reorganizing congregations, of paying the debts on her college and publishing house, and of building churches and supplying the congregations with preachers during this time. It has not yet had time to show what it may be capable of in the production of great men. Nevertheless, the attitude of the Progressives towards education has ever been friendly. The type of mind found among them is much more liberal.

Of the whole Dunker movement, truth compels one to say that it has brought forth no great literary men, and no statesman. No great poet, or philosopher, or educator was born or bred among the Dunkers during the first one hundred and fifty years of their history. But the Dunkers have produced a great mediocre class of substantial, worldly-wise, industrious, economical, peaceful, moral and religious citizens, possessed of more than the common virtues, and with few vices. They have built up, in a new land, worthy communities that feared God, were strictly honest, very hospitable, and have set an example of upright and strong manhood and womenhood.

The Dunker attitude towards education from 1790 to 1850, was due in part to oppostion they encountered from those that were educated; in part, to their frontier life and partly to the influence of tradition hostile to education. Having arrived in America, the Dunkers were confirmed in their narrowest beliefs and their dogmatic traditionalism by the isolation of their wilderness life.

However, as the wilderness began to blossom and settlements to grow together, as towns sprang up, knowledge spread; as school houses began to dot the hills, as the printing press brought to Dunker homes a part of the pulsing thought of the great world about them, introducing, at first, into their methods of farming reason instead of tradition;* as travel to and from the old home in the East gave contact with other men and other thoughts, upon some there began to dawn a recognition of certain elements of superiority in those whom they had been taught to consider as "the world". These carried back the light into the less open regions, and an ideal of rational science as opposed to dogmatic tradition, an ideal of liberty as contrasted with the ideal of unity, began to make its appeal. Then began the conflict of ideals that resulted in the ruptures of 1880-1882. After the break, familiarity with differences led to toleration, and among both the Conservatives and Progressives, toleration to liberty.

The Dunker Doctrines.

Perhaps even more striking illustrations of the Dunker type of mind than their attitude towards education, are their positions on theological and ecclesiastical questions.

In the earliest period, as we have seen, most of the Dunker doctrines were copies, or modifications, of those that were current among the sects of Europe. Their tenets today are the same as then, except as they have been affected by new circumstances.

In the strictly theological meaning of the term the Dunkers today, as in the early period of their history, have no doctrines. The decisions of the Annual Meeting, the only official pronouncements on any matter whatsoever, are not concerned with theological questions, but

*For example, until the modern era among them, the crops were planted, and all the work of the farms was governed by superstitious signs that had been handed down to them from their ancestors, instead of by the principles of scientific farming. But today they are the most scientific farmers in the world.

with conduct, organization and questions of ecclesiastical policy. The Dunkers have not declared themselves on the doctrine of God, of Man, of Sin, and of Redemption. Nothing could bring this out more clearly than to glance over a list of the subjects on which the Annual Meeting has rendered decisions.* In looking over such a list in the Index of the Revised Minutes the reader notices

*The following list from the Index of the "Revised Minutes of the Annual Meeting," which are supposed to be in force among them today reveals the type of mind that still controls the Dunkers:

"Accusations against elders; Acting as administrators of estates; Adulterers; Affirmation, objectionable forms of; Ancient order of the church, violation of; Animal shows, attending; Anointing (the sick with oil); Arbitrations, serving at; Ardent spirits; Arms, bearing; Assessor, serving as; Attorney, hiring one; Authors, playing; Avoidance; Banking, brethren engaging in; Banks, acting as directors of; Beard, style of wearing; Bells on meeting houses; Buying county bonds; Bonnets for sisters; Costly burial cases; Cape for sisters; Playing cards; Sunday school celebrations; Playing checkers; Holding office under the civil government; Clothing, plain and fashionable; Coat collar, standing; Public collections (in the church); Serving as constable; Petitioning Congress; Gospel Conversion necessary; Distilleries; Divorced persons; Dress; Getting drunk; Wearing earrings at lovefeasts; Excommunication; Fairs; Fasting; Order of faith and repentence; Following worldly fashion; Using fiddles; Fines for military service; Freemasons; Playing games; Delegates (to Annual Meeting) wearing gold; The Gospel a perfect law; Attitude to the government; Ways of wearing the hair; Wearing modest hats; Hunting on Sunday; Life Insurance; illegal interest; Selling intoxicants condemned; Jewelry; Serving on Juries; Law-suit; Going to law; Laying on of hands in baptism; Lightning rods; Having likenesses (pictures) taken; The Lord's day; Buying lottery tickets; Attending lyceums; Marriage; Military service; Mortgages; Music and musical instruments; Mustache; The New Testament our rule; Neckties; Non-conformity (to the world); Oaths; Civil office; Organs in meeting houses; Paintings in houses; Plays at parties; Pianos; Plain dressing; The Prayer Covering; Salaried ministry; Schools; Secret societies; Sleighbells; Speculation; Sunday schools; Tobacco; Erecting tombstones; Uniformity in dress; Vain conversation; Universal redemption; Going to war; Young Men's Christian Association."

These are only a part of the subjects which are given in the Index and on which the Annual Meeting has given decisions binding on the members of the Dunker church. In almost every instance, where the question is one that related to conduct, the decision is negative in its nature.

that there are just four theological subjects,—the order of faith and repentance, the Gospel a perfect law, universal redemption and the annihilation of the wicked. The whole trend of these decisions is that of a protest against practices that are held to be wicked. The chief reasons given for the positions are that such practices violate Scripture or some tradition that has been handed down, not that they are unreasonable, or evil in their effects.

Even more striking are a few quotations from the "Minutes" themselves. This one on the doctrine of the Scriptures is in point. "Art. 5, 1872.—Is the Gospel a perfect law to govern the church in all things necessary to salvation? Ans.—It is." Apologetic necessities have led the Dunkers to assert that the Bible is a divinely inspired book and that obedience is the test of love and faith.

This legalistic conception of the nature of Christianity has determined the nature of almost all the decisions of the Annual Meeting. Life is duty. The Gospel is a law of duty. How to obey this law, as well as just what this law is in its essence, has been the crux of all their troubles.

Here are examples of their deductive reasoning: "Art. 19, 1876.—Is it right, according to the Gospel, for a brother to plead the laws of the land, and act as an attorney? Ans.—The Brethren have always considered it not according to the Gospel for a brother to practive law and act as an attorney, and we can make no change in this respect".

"Art. 7, 1869,—Can a brother, consistently with the Gospel, take the benefit of the law by getting up a petition to locate a ditch according to law, and thus compel others to ditch? Ans.—We consider it most in accordance with the Gospel, and the general principles of the

Brotherhood not to use the law to compel men to do anything".

"Art. 6, 1844.—Whether it be allowable for brethren to collect debts by force of law. It was again considered that no brother has any right, in the Gospel, to sue at law. Lu. 3:14; Mt. 5:38; etc., 6:12".

"Art. 3, 1821.—How far Brethren have the liberty to commune with men who do not strictly adhere to the truth was considered in council thus: That it is very dangerous to commune with such people as do not hold entirely to the doctrine of Christ, since the Apostle says, 'If there come any unto you, and bring not this doctrine, receive him not into your house, neither bid him God-speed' (2 John 10); and the counsel is, to give them no liberty to speak in our meetings".

"Art. 4, 1845.—In regard to usury and increase, it was considered, that as it was against the law of Moses, and could not be otherwise than against the Gospel of Christ, which commands us 'to lend where we hope for nothing again', we should be very careful not to ask or take more than lawful interest, and keep an open hand for the poor, and to lend them even without interest".

These decisions are supposed to be in force among the Dunkers at the present time. It is a fact, however, that many of the decisions that stand in the "Revised Minutes" are chiefly effective in the country districts and small towns. In the larger cities and some country districts, where the isolation of the Dunkers is giving way to an unhindered communication with the other social elements, there is a tendency to allow some of the more stringent rulings to become obsolete. Moreover, the Dunker church has invented a way of rendering some of the regulations that make people conspicuous in public, less obnoxious to the rank and file of the membership.

The plan is to have such regulations apply only to the official members of the church.

Hence, on the whole the Dunker church today is somewhat further advanced in the development of the social mind than the Minutes of the Annual Meeting would suggest. The dogmatic type of mind reached its climax among them about 1880. Since that time their type of mind has gradually grown more critically intellectual. An evidence of this is the fact that the decisions of the Annual Meeting since about that time have gradually become less concerned about questions of casuistry, and have rather been directed towards completing the organization, and adapting it to the changed conditions of a new era in their history.*

*The present type of mind prevailing among the Dunkers is indicated better, perhaps, by a small circular sent out by the *Gospel Messenger*, the official publication of the church. It is as follows:

"It most earnestly pleads for a return to the apostolic order of worship and practice.

It holds that the Bible is a divinely-inspired book, and recognizes the New Testament as the only infallible rule of faith and practice for the people of God.

It also holds to the doctrine of the Trinity; teaches future rewards and punishment, and emphasizes the importance of a pure, holy and upright life before God and man.

It maintains that only those who remain faithful until death have the promise of eternal life;

That Faith, Repentance and Baptism are conditions of pardon, and hence for the remission of sins;

That Trine Immersion or dipping the candidate three times face-forward is Christian Baptism;

That Feet-Washing, as taught in John 13, is a divine command to be observed in the church;

That the Lord's Supper is a meal, and, in connection with the Communion, should be taken in the evening, or after the close of the day;

That the Salutation of the Holy Kiss, or Kiss of Charity, is binding upon the followers of Christ;

That War and Retaliation are contrary to the spirit and self-denying principles of the religion of Jesus Christ:

The Progressives have no official statement of their doctrines. In the beginning of their organization they differed from the Conservatives only on matters relating to dress, ways of wearing the hair and beard, and as to the church's power to pronounce authoritatively on questions that are not definitely settled by the Scriptures. They held that where the Scriptures do not plainly teach a certain doctrine, or custom, the church has no authority to say what a member must do. The Progressives were expelled because they refused to be obedient to the church. They held that one should obey the church only when the church has Gospel grounds for its positions, instead of the traditions of the Fathers, backed by the authority of the Annual Meeting.* Only to a minor degree was the progressive movement a revolt against the dogmatic type of mind.†

That a Nonconformity to the world in daily walk, dress, customs and conversation is essential to true holiness and Christian piety.

It maintains that in public worship, or religious exercises, Christians should appear as directed in 1 Cor. 11: 4, 5.

It also advocates the Scriptural duty of Anointing the sick with oil in the name of the Lord.

In short, it is a vindicator of all that Christ and the apostles have enjoined upon us, and aims, amid the conflicting theories and discords of modern Christendom, to point out ground that all must concede to be infallibly safe."

*See "Declaration of Principles," of the Progressives, in Holsinger, "History of the Tunkers, etc." p 530.

†Their present positions are given in a small tract that is sent out by their Publication Board at Ashland, Ohio as follows:

"In doctrine the Brethren seek unity in essentials and charity in all things, Phil. 3:13-16.

They *baptize* repentant, (Acts 2:38,) believers, (Mk. 16:16,) by *tri-une immersion* according to the commission, (Matt. 28:19; Rom. 6:3, 4; Gal. 3:27,) and confirm them by the *laying on of hands*, (Heb. 6:2; Acts 19:6,) the symbols of receiving the Spirit, (1 John 2:27.)

They keep the *communion service*, called the love-feast, (Jude 12,) with feet-washing, the symbol of cleansing, (John 13:1-17,) the *supper* teaching

In theological matters, like the Conservatives, the
Progressives have all shades of opinion. They are very
tolerant in such matters, as they have never been a
theological church. The Dunkers of all branches, true
to their origin, in German Pietism, have always been
marked by their emphasis on piety rather than orthodoxy. The latter is a word that is rarely found in the
Dunker vocabulary.

The theological doctrines held by the Progressives, as
by the Conservatives, are the result of tradition, not of
reason. Thus, even these doctrines show the same general type of mind which characterizes the Conservatives.
The only difference is that the Progressives have probably a few more men that are thinking for themselves
along theological lines than the Conservatives. But in
general the two branches are characterized by the same
general type of mind, the emotional-dogmatic, with a growing tendency to become critically-intellectual, and with
a corresponding tendency towards change in type of
character. The Progressives are only slightly in advance
of the Conservatives in these matters, at the present
day, owing to the rapid changes that have been going on
among the latter since the division in 1880-1882.

3. *The Social Organization of the Dunkers.*

The origin and development of the social organization
has already been traced. A brief sketch of the present
state of the organization is all that is necessary here.

brotherly love and equity, (1 Cor. 11:17-30,) the *eucharistic emblems*, (Luke
22:19, 20,) and kiss of love, (Rom. 16:16.) They anoint *the sick* with oil, (Jas.
5:12.) They are opposed to war, (Isa. 2:4; II Cor. 10:4; Jas. 4:1, 2,) to *oaths*,
(Matt. 6:34; Jas. 5:12;) to Brethren going to *law* with Brethren, (I Cor. 6:5
8,) to *divorce*, (Matt. 5:32; 19:9,) and to all forms of *worldliness* (John 17:15.)

The Brethren consider it their *mission* to give to the world an example
of loving and complete *obedience* to Christ and his Gospel, (John 8:31; Rom.
6:17.) They believe in primitive doctrine, purity and power."

The social composition of the Dunkers has been determined by their type of aggregation and has reacted upon it. They have always been a prolific people. From their large families, to a great extent, they have recruited the membership of the church. The Dunker family is still the primary source of their membership. However, as they become like the environing society in mind, and as the society about them, in turn, becomes affected with their ideas and customs by imitation, more and more the social composition becomes more complex. This process is now going on in most parts of the Dunker church. It is going on most rapidly in the progressive branch.

In their early history, marriage out of the church was punishable by expulsion.* It is still frowned upon, but the process of liberalization now in progress, has modified the attitude of the church. In some congregations families intermarry generation after generation. The degree of kinship is not so close that any evil results appear in the offspring, but four or five families may intermarry for a long time without being closely related. For example, I know of three families in a congregation in which the women did not change their names, when they were married; yet they and their husbands were only very distant relatives.

Occasionally, however, a Dunker marries out of the congregation. When this happens, it usually follows that the non-Dunker sooner or later joins the Dunker church. The strong social life of the Dunker family and community is so attractive that people who come in contact with them are often brought into the church, and thus new blood is introduced. For example, in the early days in Pennsylvania, the German Dunkers and the Scotch Irish immigrants mingled in the same regions, and in

*"Chronicon Ephratense ", p 96, 249 f.

many instances, the charms of the Dunker girls were too much for the Presbyterian principles of the Irish young men. Usually these men joined the Dunker church. This resulted in many Irish and Scotch names being found among the Dunkers, and in the strange phenomenon of an Irishman speaking Pennsylvania Dutch as fluently as any German. This process has been repeating itself since, wherever Dunker communities are found.

In this complexity of social composition of the Dunker membership in certain parts of the country lies a partial explanation of the coercive policy' that has been found necessary in their social organization, and the later liberalization of mind and organization. While they have always been largely a homogeneous body, there has always been just enough of heterogeneity both of ethnic elements and of ideas and social customs to compel the leaders to formulate a policy of unification. It also compelled the formulation of distinctive methods of cooperation, while at the same time, it has developed the traits of hospitality, frugality and social helpfulness so characteristic of Dunker history.

The Dunkers are a voluntary, cultural, religious association. Their constitution is based formally upon a likeness of belief, but ultimately upon a wider and more inclusive basis,—the consciousness of likeness, which includes, not only beliefs, but also like sympathies in regard to matters, aesthetic, political and economic. Their present social organization is simply a development of the single congregation, adapted to the larger problems produced by their diffusion. Except that the number of constituent societies in the church has greatly increased, the present organization does not differ from the description given in Chapter IV, for it was at that time that the final steps were taken.

Of the two lesser bodies of Dunkers the smallest is that known as the Seventh Day Baptists, which originated with Beissel, as narrated in Chapter I of Part II. The communities of this branch are gradually dying out. Their social oaganization has never been perfected, the congregations still being without organic connection.

The next larger body is the Old Order Brethren. This also is decreasing in numbers year by year. Its social organization, however, is but partially developed, as it broke away from the main body in 1880 and has undergone no further change. It represents the extremely conservative wing of the church on matters of non-conformity to the world. It is the reactionary party of modern times among the Dunkers, as Beissel's party was the reactionary party of the earlier days. The Old Order Brethren have hoped to stem the tide of development that they felt was carrying the church away from the ideals and practices of the days of isolation. They represent the element that refused to be socialized either by the progressive element in the church, or by the larger social environment outside. They have an Annual Meeting, and publish a paper at Brookville, Ohio.

The social organization of the Progressives differs from that of the Conservatives only upon the matters upon which the grievances arose at the time of the division. Three points only represent the differences between the organization of the two: (1) the general Conference of the Progressives is a body of delegates from the congregations of the denomination, although occasionally a district, too far from the place of meeting for its congregations to be represented, sends a delegate as a representative at large; (2) the Conference has no Standing

Committee.   It has an Executive Committee, which has
charge of the program for the Conference.   This differs
from the Standing Committee in that it does not decide
what matters of business shall come before the Conference, nor does it appoint committees to execute the decisions of Conference: (3) the decisions of the General
Conference are not "mandatory"; it is a body solely for
conference, and for the management of the various institutions of the church.

The social constitution of the Progressives is quite
highly developed.   It owns its own publishing house, at
Ashland, Ohio, and its college and seminary, which are
located at the same place.   It has its organized General
and Foreign Mission Boards, its young people's and its
women's societies.   Its local congregations are also
made up of several constituent societies for the division
of social labor of the congregation.

Thus, in both of the leading branches of the Dunker
church there is a developed organization.   The spirit
of these organizations is slowly becoming more liberal,
the idea that the individual exists for the church is gradually being displaced by the conception that the church
exists for the welfare of the individual.   The policy of
coercion is gradually giving way to the policy of liberal-
ism.   The ease with which constituent societies are organized in the two branches of the Dunker church at
large and in the local congregations is increasing constantly.   Ever more dominant is becoming the idea that
the only reason for the existence of the church is its ability and purpose to contribute to the welfare of men; first,
by contributing to the welfare of the individual member
of the denomination; secondly, by contributing to the
welfare of society at large by the kind of men it is able

to make of its members and send out into the larger society, the nation and the world.

Starting with eight members in 1708, the Dunkers,
Conservatives and Progressives, today number more
than one hundred thousand members. They are just beginning their career as missionizers. Hitherto they have
developed largely by pushing out from their centres of
population to the contiguous parts, and mainly by genetic
aggregation. Today they are planting missions in the
great cities of America, and in foreign lands.

Their social mind has undergone a very great change
in the last twenty five years, resulting in changes in their
doctrines and practices. Gradually they are dropping
the peculiarities that interfere with the complete expression of their main purpose of making people "good."
Education has been accepted by them, and is no
longer frowned upon as "worldly". Their religion as an
ethical force will produce men, let us hope, who, dropping
the narrowness of the old views, forsaking the isolation
of the past, and taking on the polish, the culture, the
wideness of vision and the aggressiveness of the great
world which they have shunned so long, will be of social
value in the world into which they go. The church has
shut the riches, of the "world" out from itself too long,
and it has withheld from the world the virile forces of
its own forceful, rugged moral life. If the Dunker can
adopt the best that the "world" has to give him, and yet
keep the solid strength, and the deep moral earnestness
of his past history, his individual personality will be none
the poorer, and society at large will be much the richer.
His great contribution to the social life, of which his
church is but a part, is yet to be made.

CHAPTER VII.

CONCLUSION.

Of the psychological conception of society there are four types:—the "social-contract" theory, the "impression" theory of Le Bon and Durkheim, the "imitation" theory of the late Gabriel Tarde, and the modified "instinct" theory of Professor F. H. Giddings.

The "social-contract" theory describes the last step in the organization of the Dunker church. When the original eight members had gone that far in the matter, they "consented together to enter into a covenant of a good conscience with God".* There were, however, a number of previous steps for which this theory does not account. It does not explain, for instance, why only these eight persons saw the advantages to be gained from association and were thus led, according to this theory, to form an association, or society.

The "impression" theory plays a very small part, if any, in the history of the Dunkers in this period. They were always the small party and the mass had but little influence in the decision of anyone to unite with them. It might explain why some people did not unite with them, but that is not the side of the matter that requires explanation in interpreting the origin and history of the Dunkers.

For the imitation theory more can be said. In the first two chapters attention was called to the fact that some of the events in the origin and development of the Dunkers might be explained by the historical influence of other sects. However, two things are to be noticed in this connection, (1) that this theory of historical dependence,

*"A Plain View, etc." p ix.

or of imitation, does not account for all the events and doctrines, and (2) that this theory does not answer the further question as to why the historical precedent had an influence. It is a fact that many such precedents had no influence on Mack. For example, many of the rites and doctrines of the orthodox churches and of the sects had no influence upon the Dunkers. Some other theory than that of imitation must be invoked to explain these facts. It is not denied, however, that imitation has played a very important part in the history of the Dunker people, but imitation is not the fundamental principle explaining the movement. It leaves unanswered the questions as to why one precedent and not another is imitated, and why imitation begins.

The inadequacy of the other theories to account for the Dunker history, leaves us the modified "instinct" theory of Professor Giddings. Its starting point is that the mental activity that produces society is the response of sensitive matter to a stimulus. In the like response of people to the same given stimulus we find the origin of all concerted activity, and in the unlike and unequal response is the origin of the processes of differentiation, which in their relations to the concerted activity give rise to the complex phenomena of organized society.* This theory has the advantage that it answers the questions left unanswered by the others. There is contract, conflict and imitation in every society, but the reason these processes exist is because in the ceaseless equilibration of energy between bodies unequally charged with energy some respond in a similar mannner, to the stimuli of their environment, while others respond in an unlike manner. With this fundamental formula, this theory

*See Giddings, "Concepts and Methods of Sociology", American Journal of Sociology, Vol. X, No. 2, Sept. 1904, p 164 f.

proceeds to explain under what conditions of environment like response is possible, and under what conditions impossible. The significant feature is the relation of the physical environment to the composition of the population. That is to say, the character of the physical environment determines whether the population of a country shall be homogeneous or not, while the character of the population determines its type of mind, character and disposition, its ideals, its ability to unite in concerted action and its social organization.* It is recognized in this theory that the response of individuals that gives us a society is a response to two kinds of stimuli,—(1) the stimuli of the material environment, and (2) the stimuli of the historical environment. The latter are of the greatest importance in their direct action upon the formation and history of a society. This theory we have tried, in this paper, to apply to the history of the Dunkers.

This theory explains the *origin* of the Dunkers. In Part I it was shown that Dunker doctrines, customs and organization originated in a country whose physical characteristics were such that different kinds of people settled within its borders, which physical characteristics, however, retarded the natural processes of socialization. The nature of the country was such that it attracted immigrants because of its economic opportunities, and its natural position as a highway over which people naturally traveled, while its social advantages were such as to attract the separatists persecuted in other parts of Europe. This made the demotic composition very complex, and furnished the conditions necessary for social development. The composite nature of the population determined the rise of a consciousness of unlikeness between the differ-

---

*Giddings, "A Theory of Social Causation", Publications of the American Economic Association, Third Series, vol. V, No. 2.

ing elements, and set up the processes of socialization known as conflict, toleration and imitation. The further development of consciousness of likeness within the narrow confines of Wittgenstein resulted in the emergence of ideals, of doctrines, customs and organization. The origin of the Dunker movement, therefore, is to be explained by the generalization that the environment determined the social composition, while upon the social composition depended the consciousness of kind that led to the social development.

The consciousness of kind, therefore, is the fundamental social fact that explains why the Dunkers imitated certain historical precedents and neglected others. Consciousness of likeness to the primitive Christians caused the Dunkers to go back to the New Testament, as interpreted by the primitive church, for their models of life, doctrine, custom and organization, when their consciousness of unlikeness to the people composing the membership of the state churches had caused the necessity of having a different life, doctrines, customs and organization to be felt by them. In every case, where they imitated historical precedents, they did so, because they felt that they were more like those whom they imitated than like those whom they refused to imitate. This, then, is our explanation of the sequence of events that led up to the origin of the Dunkers. Why did the Dunkers originate at all? Because certain elements in the community, conscious of a general likeness to the Pietists felt also their unlikeness to the latter on the point of the necessity of separation from the state churches, and of discipline to make separation possible. Why did they feel this unlikeness? Because the social composition of the Pietistic groups as a whole lacked perfect homogeneity, and this, because in their evolution they had inherited different tendencies, and had been subjected to slightly different environmental conditions. They had lived in different districts, read different books, had occupied unlike positions in life, and had had unlike experiences.

After the Dunker ideals had once arisen and had got themselves incarnated in the persons of the first eight members, a new social stimulus had come into existence for those about them that were not yet members of their organization. This was a secondary stimulus, an ideal. To it men responded according to the completeness of their mental and moral likeness to the Dunker type. If they were conscious of their likeness to the Dunkers, they united with the latter. If, on the other hand, they were conscious of being unlike the Dunkers, they not only remained outside the Dunker organization, but became animated with a hostility to it and its members. In either case the decision tended to confirm people in their attitude. Thus, differentiation became greater and finally permanent. The removal to America and consequent decay of the sect in Europe was due to the lack of assimilation in the districts where the Dunker congregations were located. The decay of the congregation at Crefeld was due to lack of social assimilation of the elements that composed it; that at Schwarzenau to the introduction of social heterogeneity into the population of Wittgenstein.

The origin of the sect in America was due, as we saw, to a greater complexity of causes. It began with a consciousness of unlikeness to the elements of the social population at Germantown, made apparent by the close contact of the Dunkers with the other elements located there. It was complicated, however, by the fact that Becker and many of his fellow settlers had been Dunkers in Germany, and therefore imitated the Dunkers there, when the social situation at Germantown had suggested the need of a new social organization.

Consciousness of kind determined the course of the early history in America. The character of the country about Philadelphia had made very complex the social population settled there. The environments of Germantown and Conestoga were different and had much to do with the different ideals of Beissel and Becker. The resulting differences of ideals made the two parties recognize their unlikenesses, and finally determined their permanent separation. Lack of communication and association had meanwhile hindered the process of socialization.

It was noticed how the economic opportunities of new regions together with consciousness of kind account for the expansion of the Dunkers and its direction.

This expansion stopped the process of socialization that had just begun, and lack of communication between the different congregations gave rise to variations in Dunker doctrines, customs, and forms of organization.

With the growth of the country industrially, with the increase of means of communication, there arose a consciousness of these variations, and a desire in some Dunker minds to remove them. This gave rise to the ideal of uniformity. In the effort to realize that ideal there originated the great development in doctrine and organization that characterized the history of the Dunker church from 1835 to 1880-1882. It also gave rise to the policy of coercion in regard to the individual, that we saw in the same period. This process of unification, or centralization, reached its zenith in 1882.

It was observed, furthermore, that with the development of means of communication and association there set in another tendency. The great environing society began to make itself felt upon the social life of the Dunkers. The larger socializing process had begun. There began to develop a consciousness of kind between the Dunkers and the other social elements about them. This gave rise to the liberalization of the Dunker church.

In every step of this development we have noticed the causes. The whole movement was conditioned by the physical nature of the country. The fundamental social fact in the origin and development of the Dunkers was a consciousness of kind. That had been determined by the physical character of the country along the Rhine in Germany, which had allowed various elements to congregate there. Likewise, in America that which developed the consciousness among the Dunkers that they were more alike than they were like the other elements of the population here, was the fact that the country was of such a nature that it attracted many kinds of people from different nations and regions. This was repeated, when the Dunkers spread out over what is now the United States. On the other hand, the physical nature of the United States was such that the elements that congregated here in its early history, possessed potential resemblance. That fact determined that American society should be progressive, one in which the various elements should gradually be socialized. The socialization is simply a part of that great process that is still in progress.

BIBLIOGRAPHY.

ACRELIUS, "History of New Sweden". (Valuable for the light it throws upon the situation in early Pennsylvania and New Jersey, and especially for its account of his visit to Beissel at Ephrata.)

JOHN ARNDT, "True Chrisnianity". (Throws light on the ideas prevalent among certain sectarians of Germany).

GOTTFRIED ARNOLD, "Unpartaische Kirchen—und Ketzer Historien, etc."
    "   "   "Die Erste Liebe".
(Both are valuable as sources of information about the parties and beliefs current among them in Germany at the time of the origin of the Dunkers).

T. C. BANFIELD, "Industry on the Rhine,—Agriculture". London, 1846.

ROBERT BARCLAY, "Apology for the Quakers".
    "   "   "A Catechism and Confession of Faith".
    "   "   "Religious Societies of the Commonwealth".

B. BAUER, "Der Einfluss des Englischen Quakerthum auf die deutsche Cultur, u. s. w."

WILLIAM BAUER, "Religious Life in Germany during the Wars of Indepedence".

SAMUEL BOWNAS, "An Account of the Life, Travels and Christian Experiences in the Work of the Ministry of Samuel Bownas".

M. G. BRUMBAUGH, "History of the Brethren".

A. BRONS, "Ursprung, Entwickelung und Shicksale der Taufgesinnten, oder Mennonites, etc."

T. F. CHAMBERS, "Early Germans of New Jersey".

S. H. COBB, "Story of the Palatines".
    "   "   "Palatine or German Immigration to New York and Pennsylvania".

C. A. CORNELIUS, "Die Niederlandischen Widertaeufer, u. s. w."
    "   "   "Geschichte des Muensterischen Aufruhrs, Part II, "Die Widertaufe".

DANKER AND SCHLUYTER, "Journal". (Translated by H. C. Mur-hpy in Vol. I of the Memoirs or the Long Island Historical Society. Valuable for the light it throws upon the customs and habits of the people of America, especially for the Laba-dists of Maryland).

JOHN DICKINSON, "Letters from a Farmer in Pennsylvania to the Inhabitants of the British Colonies." (Valuable for the insight it affords into the thoughts and customs of the com-mon people of Pennsylvania at an early day).

F. DIBELIUS, "Gottfried Arnold, sein Leben und seine Bedeutung fur Kirche und Theologie".

F. R. DIFFENDERFER, "The Palatine and Quaker as Common-wealth Builders".

"   "   "The German Exodus to England in 1709." (Pennsylvania German Society Proceedings, vol. 17.)

"   "   "German Immigration into Pennsylvania".

JOS. H. DUBBS, "Founding of the German Churches of Penn-sylvania" (Pennsylvania Magazine of Biography and His-tory, vol. 17.)

MORGAN EDWARDS, "Materials towards a History of the Baptists in America". (Very important for a knowledge of the early Dunker congregations in America).

FISHER, "The Making of Pennsylvania; an Analysis of the Ele-ments of its Population".

JOHN FISKE, "Dutch and Quaker Colonies in America".

"   "   "Old Virginia and her Neighbors".

GEORGE FOX, "Journal".

K. F. GEISER, "Redemptioners and Indented Servants, etc."

P. E. GIBBONS, "Pennsylvania Dutch, and other Essays".

MAX GOEBEL, "Die Geschichte des Christlichen Lebens in der rhenisch-westphaelischen, evangelischen Kirche". (Very valuable for a knowledge of religious conditions in the Rhine valley in the period in which the Dunkers originated).

J. I. GOOD, "History of the Reformed Church in Germany, 1620—1890".

"Historisch—Topographisch—Statistiche Beschreibung der Stadt Gersheim". (No author given; In Union Theological Seminary Library, New York City).

"German American Annals", vol. 1—12. (Published by the German American Society, Philadelphia, Penna).

L. HAEUSSER, "Geschichte der rhenischen Pfalz." (Very valuable).

"Hallische Nachrichten, etc., 1787". (These are reports of the United Evangelical Churches in Pennsylvania at that time, and are very valuable).

HENDERSON, "A Short History of Germany", 2 vols.

A. HARNACK, "History of Dogma", vol. 7.

C. R. HILDEBURN, "Issues of the Press in Pennsylvania, 1685—1784". 2 vols. (Very valuable for a knowledge of the sources for the American period).

H. R. HOLSINGER, "History of the Tunkers and of the Brethren Church". (Very important for the divisions in the Dunker church in its later history).

O. KUHNS, "German and Swiss Settlements of Colonial Pennsylvania". (One of the best small books on these settlements).

KARL LAMPRECHT, "Deutsche Geschichte", 7 vols.

"List of Works relating to the Germans in the United States in the Library of Congress". Compiled by A. P. C. Griffen, Chief Bibliographer, Washington.

D. MILLER, "Pennsylvania German". (A collection of Prose and Poetry in the dialect).

MENNO SYMONS, "Opera Omnia Theologica". Amsterdam: 1681. (In Dutch).

"Gottlieb Mittelberger's Journey to Pennsylvania in the year 1750, and Return to Germany in the Year 1754, etc.", translated by Eben, Philadelphia, 1898.

A. C. Myers, "Immigration of the Irish Quakers into Pennsylvania, 1682—1750".

S. B. O'Callaghan, "Documentary History of New York".

Oncken, "Allgemeine Geschichte: Zeitalter des Friedrichs d. Grossen".

F. D. Pastorius, "A Particular Geographical Description of the Lately Discovered Province of Pennsylvania". (Memoirs of the Historical Society of Pennsylvania, vol. 4, Prt. 2, 1850.)

"Penn's and Logan's Correspondence". (Ibid, vols. 9, I0.)

Penn, "Select Works". 3 vols.

Penn, "Works". 2 vols.

"Pennsylvania, the German Influence in its Settlement and Development. Prepared by the authority of the Penmsylvania German Society". 2 vols.

S. W. Pennypacker, "The Pennsylvania Dutchman, and wherein he excelled".

  "   " "The Settlement of Germantown".

  "   " "Johann Gottfried Seelig, and the Hymn Book of the Hermits of the Wissahickon". (In Pennsylvania Magazine of History and Biography. Also printed separately).

  "   " "Historical and Biographical Sketches". (All of these are of considerable importance).

I. D. Rupp, "History of Lancaster County".

  "   " "He Pasa Ecclesia. An Original History of the Religious Denominations existing at present in the United States". Philadelphia: 1844.

  "   " "Early History of Pennsylvania, etc."

B. Rush, "Historical Notes of Dr. B. Rush, 1777", edited by Dr· S. Weir Mitchell. (Also to be found in Penna. Mag. History and Biog., April, 1903).

J. F. Sachse, "The Fatherland, 1450—1700, showing the part it bore in the discovery, exploration and development, etc., of

Pennsylvania". (In Pennsylvania German Society Proceedings and Addresses, vol. 7).

ALVIN SCHULTZ, "Das haeusliche Leben der europaeischen Kulturvoelker, von Mittelalter bis zur zweiten Haelfte des 18 Jahrhunderts". (Valuable on the details of dress and other customs in the period of the origin of the Dunkers).

O. SEIDENSTICHER, "The First Century of German Printing in America, 1723—1830".

"   "   "Germans in Pennsylvania".

"   "   "Bilder aus der deutsch–Pennsylvanischen Geschichte, etc".

"   "   "Die Erste Einwanderung in America und die Grundung von Germautown im Jahre 1683, etc."

"   "   "Ephrata: eine Amer. Klostergeschiehte". (All these by Seidensticher are of great value).

WM. SEWELL, "History of the Rise and Progress of the People called Quakers".

C. G. SOWER, "Bishop Christopher Sower of Germantown".

P. J. SPENER, "Werke".

ROBERT TODD, "Robert Hunter and the Settlement of the Palatines". (In the Memorial History of the City of New York, vol. 2, chapter 4).

J. W. WAYLAND, "The Germans of the Valley". (In the Virginia Magazine of History and Biography, vol. 9).

H. F. WAKEMAN, "Europe from 1598—1715".

SPECIAL SOURCES.

Besides the above of more general interest to the student of Dunker history, the following books and periodicals are of special value, and have been used largely in the preparation of the dissertation.

A. MACK, "A Plain View of the Rites and Ordinances of the House of God, arranged in the form of a Conversation between a Father and Son, to which are added Ground-

Searching Questions, answered by the Author''.

(A translation of ''Kurz und Einfaeltige Vorstellung der aeussern aber doch heiligen Rechten und Ordnungen des Hauses Gottes, u. s. w.'', a copy of which is to be found in the Library of the Historical Society of Pennsylvania. This is quite a good translation. It is published by the Brethren Publishing Co., Elgin, Ill.)

CHRISTOPHER SAUER, *''Almanacs''*.

    ''   '' *''Sendschreiber''*.

    ''   '' *''Geistliche Magazin''*. (Some numbers missing). (All of these are to be found in the Library of the Penna. His. Soc.)

CONRAD BEISSEL, ''Zeugnisse''.

    ''   '' ''Mystische und Erfahrungs–volle Episteln''.

(Both of these are bound in one volume, now in the Library of Union Theological Seminary, New York).

Brothers LAMECH and AGRIPPA, ''Chronicon Ephratense'', translated into English by Dr. Max Hark.

GEORGE ADAM MARTIN, ''Christliche Bibliothek''. (In Penna. His. Soc. Library).

VAN BRAGHT, ''Der Bluetige Schau–Platz'', or, Rupp's translation, ''The Bloody Mirror''.

''The Berleberg Bible'', edited by Mack and Hochman, and other Pietists.

''The Classified Minutes of the Annual Meeting''.

''The Revised Minutes of the Annual Meeting''.

''Geistliche Fama''. (A periodical in the Library of the Historical Society of Pennsylvania. '')

''Minutes and Letters of the Coetus of Pennsylvania, 1734— 1792''.

Files of the *Gospel Messenger, Progressive Christian, Brethren Evangelist, Brethren Family Almanac, The Brethren Annual*, and some minor publications of the different branches of the church.

VITA.

The writer was born Oct. 12, 1871 in Black Hawk County, Iowa.
He attended the public schools there and in Linn county Iowa.
After a year in the preparatory department of Upper Iowa
University, at Fayette, he taught school, and subsequently
entered the College at Upper Iowa University, from which he
received the degree of Bachelor of Literature. He then went to
Iowa College at Grinnell, Iowa, where he received the degree of
Bachelor of Arts. He then served as pastor of the Brethren
Church at Waterloo, Iowa for six years. In 1903 he received
the degree of Master of Arts in Columbia University, his thesis
being on "The Pennsylvania Dutch Settlement of Orange Township, Black Hawk County, Iowa, a Paper in Descriptive Sociology". In 1904 he received the degree of Bachelor of Divinity
in the Union Theological Seminary, New York, his thesis being
on, "A Critical Comparison of the Creeds of the Ancient Church
Orders". In 1904 he was awarded the "Hitchcock Prize in
Church History" in Union Theological Seminary, New York.